Poet Lore, A Magazine Of Letters: Spring, 1916

Charlotte Porter

ESTABLISHED 1889

THE OLDEST AND LARGEST REVIEW IN THE ENGLISH LANGUAGE

DEVOTED TO POETRY AND DRAMA

Poet Lore

TITLE REGISTERED AS A TRADE MARK

A Magazine of Letters

Spring Number

The Poet Lore Company
Publishers
194 Boylston St   Boston U.S.A.

Poet Lore

Editors: CHARLOTTE PORTER and HELEN A. CLARKE

MARCH–APRIL, 1916

NOTICE TO SUBSCRIBERS.

POET LORE is published bi-monthly in the months of January (*New Year's Number*), March (*Spring Number*), May (*Summer Number*), July (*Vacation Number*), September (*Autumn Number*), and December (*Winter Number*). Subscribers not receiving their copies by the end of these months should immediately notify the publishers, who otherwise cannot agree to supply missing numbers.

Annual subscriptions $5.00. Single copies $1.00. As the publishers find that the majority of subscribers desire unbroken volumes, POET LORE WILL BE SENT UNTIL ORDERED DISCONTINUED AND ALL ARREARS PAID.

Poet Lore

VOLUME XXVII (March 1916)   SPRING, 1916   NUMBER II

GRINGOIRE

Comedy By Théodore de Banville

Translated from the French by Arthur B. Myrick, Ph. D.

Dramatis Personae

Louis XI, *King of France (forty-six years old).*
Pierre Gringoire, *poet, (twenty).*
Simon Fourniez, *merchant, (forty-eight).*
Olivier-le-Daim, *the King's barber.*
Loyse, *daughter of* Simon Fourniez, *(seventeen).*
Nicole Andry, *sister of* Simon Fourniez, *(twenty-four).*
King's Pages, Servants of Simon Fourniez, Officers and
     Archers of the Scotch Guard

Scene at Tours, in the house of Simon Fourniez, *in the month of March, of the year 1469.*

The stage represents a fine Gothic chamber, furnished with the serious luxury of the wealthy bourgeoisie. The rear of the stage is occupied by a large stone fireplace with fluted columns in clusters, ornamented with three figurines set on brackets. On each side of the fireplace a door with two panels, forming a part of the oaken wainscoting covering the walls half way up. These doors open on a stair-landing lighted by two trefoil-shaped windows, rather low set, with little lozenge panes. Ceiling with painted beams, studded with pewter rosettes. In the side-walls two windows with deep embrasures, hung with serge curtains. To the left, a large dresser, with three shelves and projecting canopies, laden with silver plate and dishes delightful to gaze upon. To the right, a brass clock, whose works, hammer and chime are visible. On the floor, a thick mat of esparte grass. High-backed chairs, square table and oaken stools.

As the curtain rises, OLIVIER-LE-DAIM *is standing by the window to the right. Two of the King's pages stand motionless before the dresser.* LOUIS XI, *sitting in a large carved chair, stuffed with scarlet and gold cushions.* SIMON FOURNIEZ *and* NICOLE ANDRY *are sitting about a table still laden with fruits and silver wine-jugs.* NICOLE, *as she finishes a tale she has just been telling, rises to pour the King some wine.*

SCENE I

Nicole.—Yes, Sire, so it is that in the reign of the late King your father, the demoiselle Godegrand married a man hanged, whom some scholars had cut down by way of jest, and deposited in the old spinster's chamber while she was at vespers.

The King (laughing).—An excellent jest. Master Olivier-le-Daim, what do you say to this merry story?

Olivier.—I should say, Sire, that the young man had been badly hanged.

The King.—Naturally. Thou dost ever hit the nail on the head at once. (*To* NICOLE.) Never mind, 'tis a merry enough tale. It is a pleasure to listen to you, fair Nicole. Why do you stand so far from me?

Nicole.—For respect, Sire.

The King.—Come here.

Nicole.—I should not dare.

The King.—Well! *I* shall dare!

Nicole.—Oh! Sire!

The King.—About how old are you?

Nicole.—I am twenty-four, Sire.

The King.—'Tis no good age to be left a widow. Especially when one is the most blooming beauty in our good city of Tours. Are you not called everywhere the fair draper's wife?

Nicole.—Oh! Sire! so they call me because I was hailed by that name in a song that has become famous in the long winter evenings.

The King.—And who wrote this song? Some lover of those sly eyes?

Nicole.—A lover! Oh! no, Sire. 'Twas Gringoire!

The King.—What do you mean by Gringoire?

Olivier.—A nobody, Sire.

Simon.—An actor, a very jovial, droll fellow. Upon my word, he's the wildest and the hungriest of all starveling poets.

The King.—Which apparently does not prevent him from being a good judge of lovely women and praising triumphantly the fairest of all.

Nicole (to SIMON FOURNIEZ*).*—Don't you see that the King is making love to me? Defend me, brother!

Simon.—Oh! our lord King loves to jest, but thou art an honest woman and thou canst defend thyself.

Nicole.—Then, Sire, permit me to drink to him who punishes expressly in this realm all cheats of good repute and thieves of honour!

The King (pressing NICOLE*).*—Ah! this is treason, I must avenge myself.

Nicole (kneeling before the King and raising her glass).—I drink to the King's health! to his long life!

The King (checking himself).—Against a woman's wit, the devil's wiles are weak.

Nicole.—To his triumph over all his enemies!

The King.—By heaven! the cruelest of all, are those eyes that burn me like the fire of hell! But what stratagem can I use against an enemy that paralyses both my attack and pursuit? Will it be said that King Louis was afraid?

Nicole.—If any one should say that, the English of Dieppe and the Swiss of Bâle might answer that he lied.

Simon.—Well said, sister. And if the King is the most valiant captain in his realm, he is also its justest lord, and perhaps most modest. That is why I dare to thank him for the favour he has deigned to grant us in sitting down at table in the house of one of his burghers.

The King.—Say, of one of his friends, Simon Fourniez. Thou art for me no mere burgher and chance acquaintance. I have not forgotten the pleasant hours that I have passed in thy garden, that very garden about this friendly house, when I was as yet but Dauphin of France. At that most cruel moment, when, at my own expense, I served the hard apprenticeship of life, thou, faithful and humble servant, helped me with thy purse; nay further, thou didst risk thy life for me. And how, I know! These are memories that nothing can efface, good and worthy friend Simon. To say nothing of the fact that thy daughter Loyse is my god-daughter!

Simon.—Ah! Sire, pardon me. I weep with joy. *I* did not wait to devote myself to you, until you were King and all powerful master, for it took us but a moment to understand each other! A burgher born among the people, feeling and thinking as they did, I guessed with what ardour you loved our poor quarrel-rent land. Now, a chief was needed, a chief with a heavy but valiant hand, who should be a father to us all, an inflexible master to the shepherds that sheared our wool too close. You were our man and we understood you!

The King.—'Tis the right way to speak. By Heaven! Simon Fourniez, thou art right, my people and my burghers are what I prefer to all. If I have come to-day to ask thee a supper, it is because, thank God, I may at last snatch a bit of rest: I have won the right to it! Till this evening I desire to rejoice freely in your company and treat myself to the pleasure of no longer being King. The sorry days of Péronne and Liége have passed, my friends! (*Rubbing his hands.*) Mon cousin of Burgundy is wasting his time in the duchy of Gueldres and the landgraviate of Alsace!

Nicole.—But men swear the sly fellow desires to establish in Champagne my lord your brother of Normandy——

Simon.—To provide himself a road between his Ardennes and his Burgundy!

The King.—Yes, there has been talk of that. Oh! duke Charles is shrewd and crafty!

Simon (*with a glance at the King*).—But they may find a shrewder and craftier one than he!

The King.—What wouldst thou say, friend Simon, if by renouncing Champagne, my brother should receive from me in fair exchange the provinces of Guyenne and Aquitaine?

Simon.—I should say that it would be an excellent trick!

The King.—And a good exchange! For a young man, a lover of pleasure, as is my lord brother. So he will certainly not refuse.

Olivier (*stepping forward*).—You believe so, Sire?

The King.—Do I think so, Olivier? (*Taking a swallow of wine.*) La Balue I charged with the business. I count on La Balue: A faithful servant, he.

Olivier.—So faithful that the King will not be long in being surprised by him!

The King (setting down his glass).—What dost thou mean?

Olivier.—I, Sire? Nothing. *(Aside)* Let us leave him his good humour. I need it.

The King (rising and approaching him).—What is it then, Master Olivier? What have you to mutter thus between your teeth? Will you deny perchance that I hold the cards in my own hand, and that the advantage has turned to me?

Olivier.—No, Sire. It would have been unnatural for the shrewdest player to lose forever!

The King.—So I shall sweep the board, my friends. Come, let's rejoice, Simon, and pour us thy good old wine which is the ruddy blood of fair Touraine.

Simon (filling the King's glass).—'Tis yours, Sire!

(Servants and pages carry the table to a corner of the hall and prepare the King's arm-chair.

The King (after drinking).—And now I shall show thee that, if thou lovest me, thou hast not to deal with any ingrate.

Simon.—Ah! Sire!

The King.—War is not all, my friend. Commerce, you know, is as well the might of a nation. Now, I have important interests to discuss with my friends, the Flemish.

Simon.—Good!

The King (seating himself).—And it has occurred to me to make thee my ambassador.

Simon.—Ambassador! I! Your Majesty has deigned to think of me for such a mission! Why! it is impossible; I cannot talk in proper terms to lords.

The King.—It is not with nobles that thou art to negotiate but with hosiers and brass beaters. Better than any other shalt thou do my business.

Simon (embarrassed).—Yes—but my shop, Sire?

The King.—Good! It is the best patronised in the whole town! At a pinch thy goods should sell themselves.

Nicole.—Sire, I can hasard a shrewd guess at my brother's thought. It is not his trade that disturbs him; it is Loyse whom he would dare confide to none, not even to you, not even to me.

Simon.—If only Loyse were married!

The King.—She need not be an obstacle. Let's marry her.

Simon.—If Your Majesty thinks that it is easy! I have never cherished any desire but that. But Loyse is obstinate about it and until now she has resisted.

The King.—Perhaps I shall have more influence over her.

Simon.—But besides we should have to find her a husband!

Olivier (*approaching*).—But that is not the difficulty, Master Simon. Is not the demoiselle Loyse as pretty as a little fairy?

The King (*looking at Olivier*).—Thou hast noticed it?

Olivier.—Who would not, unless he were blind?

The King.—A just observation. And to this charm of gentleness and beauty, Loyse adds others still. She has a father who owns fields——

Simon.—Superb fields!

The King.—Vineyards——

Simon.—That produce the best wine in Tours!

The King.—And on the neighbouring hillsides——

Simon.—Many a fine mill that the wind will never leave still.

The King.—Then, too, Loyse is our god-daughter. She is a good match.

Simon.—A splendid match for some rich burgher of our good town. That is what I tell her every day. But she will not listen to me.

Olivier.—Suppose you should offer her something better?

Simon (*offended*).—Better than a burgher!

The King (*ironically*).—Thou dost not guess, Simon? Master Olivier, to be sure, who after a youth, filled with toil and adventure, seems, I think, very desirous of making an end!

Simon (*affecting modesty*).—Such an end is not worthy of your barber, Sire! Providence, doubtless, holds a better in store for him.

Olivier.—Eh!

Simon (*good humouredly*).—I say what everyone says.

The King.—Well! We shall consult Loyse herself. Be easy, friend, I have done more difficult things. But, by the way, what has become of my gentle Loyse? Is she out of patience with us? I long, however, to see her smile, and to listen to her dainty chatter!

Simon.—Here, Sire, here she is. It seems as if she had guessed Your Majesty's desire—and mine.

SCENE II

The King (*smiling benevolently at Loyse who enters*).—Thou art here, my Loyse?

Loyse (*kneeling on a cushion at the King's feet*).—Yes, Sire. I did not forget you!

The King.—Dost thou know what friend Simon was saying to me? He claimed that thou wert as completely devoted to me as to him, and that, just as to him, thou canst not refuse me anything in the world.

Loyse.—Try, Sire.

The King (taking her head between his hands and looking at her affectionately).—Listen. I desire that thou shouldst be content. There is no one thing to which I attach more weight, for (*confidentially*). I have never told thee, (*gravely*) if the stars lie, not, I have good reasons for believing that my happiness is bound up with thine.

Loyse (enthusiastically).—Then make *me* happy at once!

The King (apart).—Dear dove-like soul! (*To* Loyse.) Wilt thou obey me?

Loyse.—Oh! with all my heart.

The King.—Well! my darling, thou must marry.

Loyse.—So that is what you wanted to ask me?

The King.—Yes.

Loyse (regretfully).—Oh! what a pity!

The King.—And why so, dear child? Thou art a grown girl, pretty and rosy as flowering April; such a treasure cannot remain without a master. Say one word, and thou shalt have the most generous merchant in Tours! Thou dost smile? I think I understand thee. The drapers and merchants of our good town have lands, sunny vineyards, but they have too, for the most part, white hair and stooped shoulders. And he of whom thou dost think when thou art all alone, is a young apprentice with blond hair who has nought but his yardstick! That is no hindrance. By the Virgin! I shall so enrich the apprentice that he may feast his old master on a thick napped cloth, in good and solid plate. So, name him fearlessly.

Loyse.—Sire, I care no more for an apprentice than a merchant.

Simon (angrily).—Perhaps thou dost think us of too base lineage for thee!

Loyse.—It is not for me to depreciate the calling that my father follows so honourably.

Simon.—Well, then?

Loyse (continuing).—But I see no difference between a shop and a prison. What! to sit so in this darkness, in this vexation of spirit, when the world is so wide, when there are so many skies and lands, so many rivers and stars!

The King.—Thou wilt not have a merchant?—Thou art silent?

Loyse.—Sire——

Nicole.—Fear not, Sire. Loyse tells me everything and I shall question her well.

Loyse.—I have no secrets, aunt. The King knows well my mother was the daughter of a draper of Tours. As a little child, playing along the banks of the Loire, she was carried off by gypsies. Twelve years later they found her as by a miracle, still good, virtuous and sweet, but the love of living in the open air and a yearning for infinite space was hers for the remnant of her wandering life. My good father married her with sincere love and made her happy——

Simon.—My poor wife!

Loyse.—And yet she died young, although surrounded by care and love. She was always thinking of those happy countries where fruits and flowers burst forth together in the light. I have in *my* veins my mother's blood: that is why, Sire, I will not marry a merchant.

Simon.—Princess!

The King.—Wilt thou have a soldier?

Loyse.—No, Sire. To stay at home when my husband might be meeting the risks and dangers of battle! Would that not be basely enduring a separate torture every moment?

The King.—So thy heart says nothing?

Nicole (to the King).—Nothing, Sire.

Loyse (simply).—Yes it does. But what it tells me is very confused. (*She quietly approaches the King and pensively rests her head on the chair in which he is sitting.*) It seems to me that I love a man who, of course, has no existence, since I would have him as valiant as a captain and capable of heroic deeds, but gentle as a woman. Fancy whether my day-dreams are mad! When I think of this unknown lover, I often see him ill and wretched, needing my protection, as if I were his mother! You see certainly that I am a little girl, not even knowing what she wills, and you must give me more time to read my mind more clearly.

Simon.—As well give a cat time to unwind a ball of yarn! Ah! thou wilt not have a husband! Well, I promise thee one thing, that thou shalt have one before long.

Loyse.—No, father, leave me free, with my flowers, in the open air and broad sunlight!

Simon (*outraged*).—In the broad sunlight! (*To the King.*)
Sire, order her to obey me.

The King.—Ah! Simon, here I am not the King!

Loyse (*coaxing*).—Good father, keep me here, do not drive
me away.

Simon.—There! Do you know what I shall finally do, some
fine day? I shall lock thee safely in thy chamber, and thou shall
come out only when thou hast submitted to my will.

Loyse (*with a curtsey*).—Don't be angry, father. I shall go
myself. I shall go immediately, but (*clasping her hands*) do not
marry me. (*To the King.*) Good-bye, god-father!

The King.—Poor Loyse! (*Exit* LOYSE *with a childlike and
mutinous grace.*)

SCENE III

The King.—Thou hast put her to flight, Simon!

Simon.—I *will* exact obedience from her! It is for me to
show firmness, since Your Majesty would persuade your god-
daughter to be happy!

The King.—Bah! People no more like to have happi-
ness from other people's hands than eels to be skinned alive!

Olivier.—Those of whom Your Majesty speaks are ingrates!

The King.—You might as well say everybody!

Simon.—Ah! Sire, I am a mistreated father. Farewell my
embassy! I shall never see your coppersmiths.

The King.—Calm thyself. Loyse's refusal depends merely
upon the fact that as yet she loves no one. We need only seek
the man she can love.

Nicole (*to the King*).—And our Loyse will hardly be so anx-
ious to see far away lands on that day when some one has become
the whole world to her!

The King.—Good! But still we must find this some one.
(*Outside is heard a great uproar and prolonged bursts of laughter.*)
What is this tumult? (SIMON FOURNIEZ *goes to the window at the
right, and suddenly bursts into laughter.*) What is it then?

Simon (*laughing*).—Sire, it is Gringoire!

Olivier (*aside*).—Gringoire! Here! The clowns let him
come near this place!

Simon.—Oh! there he is in front of the shop of my neighbour,
the pastry cook. His eyes seem as if they would take the well-
browned chickens from their hooks. He devours their aroma,
Sire! My faith, Gringoire is an odd fellow, to be sure.

Olivier (*to* SIMON FOURNIEZ).—Yes, and this odd fellow often stops beneath the windows of your house, especially under your daughter's.

Nicole.—Where is the harm?

Simon.—He has such good songs! (*He sings.*)

"Satan with us plays the barber!   "Satan chez nous s'est fait barbier!
The razor he   Il tient le rasoir—"

(*Meeting the glance of* OLIVIER-LE-DAIM, *and finishing between his teeth.*)

"grips in his claw!"   "dans sa griffe!"

(*Aside*). Oh! the devil! I forgot!

Olivier.—So it seems that these songs are listened to here?

Nicole (*boldly*).—Of course.

Olivier.—Take care. You should not boast of it too much.

The King.—Why so?

Olivier.—Because among these brazen songs that have respect for none——

The King.—Ah! I see.

Olivier (*continuing*).—There is a certain "Ballad of the Hanged," as it is called, which should win the rope for him who wrote it.

Nicole (*aside, in terror*).—The rope!

The King.—What! Nicole, is it this good fellow of whom you told me who so arouses the whole populace?

Simon (*to the King*).—Does he even know what he does? Gringoire, Sire, is a child.

Olivier.—A wicked and a dangerous child like all his ilk! Rhymers are a sort of madmen not shut up, I know not why, although the sanest of them sups on moonshine, and behaves with less judgment than a tame beast.

Nicole (*indignant.*—Oh! (*To the King.*) Is it true, Sire?

The King.—Not quite, and Master Olivier-le-Daim is a trifle too proud. You seem, Nicole, to be keenly interested in this rhymer, who has sung your charms?

Nicole.—Yes, Sire. I admit boldly that I like him.

The King.—You like him?

Nicole.—Cordially. And if Gringoire were not as proud as the emperor of the Turks, he would have always a seat by the hearth and a good meal in our house. When I saw him for the first time, it was three years ago, in the harsh winter we had then, when for two months, the ground was all white with snow. Grin-

goire was sitting under the porch of a house in the rue du Cygne;
he had on his knees two little lost children, whom he had found
crying for their mother and shivering with cold. He had stripped
his own sorry doublet off his shoulders to wrap them in, and half-
naked as he was, he was lulling the little ones to sleep, singing
them a hymn of the Holy Virgin.

The King (after reflecting).—I will see this Gringoire.

Olivier.—Ah!

Nicole.—Ah! Sire! 'Tis a kingly thought you have.
Poor fellow! See now, he is already triumphing over his star!

Olivier.—Call such a mountebank before the King!

The King.—I have said! I wish it.

Olivier (changing his mind).—So be it! (*He bows before the
King, and goes and gives an order to the officers placed in the next
room.*)

The King.—This diversion is as good as another. And I
think there is no feast excellent, an it come not to an end with
some good drollery and jest.

Simon.—That is my opinion. Gringoire will recite one of
his farces—one of the spicy ones! The farce of Pathelin, for
example,—Baa, baa, baa!

Olivier (to the King).—Your Majesty will be obeyed. Grin-
goire will come and I shall make him repeat a few rhymes. Only,
I cannot be sure that they will amuse Your Majesty!

The King.—We shall see! and provided his songs be less
evil than thou dost pretend, since Gringoire is so starved, we have
enough here to feast him. (*Dishes are placed on the table.*) That
will not displease him.

Simon (going to the door).—Here he is.

Scene IV

Enter Gringoire *escorted by archers, pale, shivering and
almost staggering with hunger.*

Gringoire.—Ah! come now, master archers, where are you
taking me? (*To the archers.*) Why this violence? (*The archers
are silent.*) These are Scottish men at arms who have no French.
(*At a sign from* Olivier-le-Daim *the archers release* Gringoire,
and go out as well as the pages.) Eh? They loose me now!
(*Perceiving the King and* Olivier-le-Daim.) Who are these
gentlemen? (*Sniffing the aroma of the repast.*) All-powerful

God, what fragrance! So I was brought to sup? I was brought
by force to eat a good dinner! Force was idle. I should have
come with a good will. (*Admiring the arrangement of the repast.*)
Pasties, venison, jugs full of good sparkling wine! (*To the King
and* OLIVIER-LE-DAIM.) I guess it, you realised that these
archers were haling me off to prison without my having supped,
and then you sent for me to get me out of their clutches—their
hands I mean, and to give me hospitality as the potters did to
Homer!

The King.—Do you tell the truth, Master Gringoire? You
have not yet supped?

Gringoire.—Supped? No sir. Not to-day.

Nicole (*approaching the King*).—That is evident. See his
lean, wan face.

Gringoire.—Madame Nicole Andry!

Simon (*stepping forward*).—He is starving to death.

Gringoire.—Master Simon Fourniez! In my confusion I
did not at first recognize your house.

Olivier (*to* GRINGOIRE).—You have not supped? Well then,
will you please accept a wing of this fowl?

Gringoire (*as if in a daze*).—Yes. Two wings. And a leg!

Olivier.—There's a vineyard wine that would enliven a
dead man.

Gringoire (*moving up to the table*).—That's what I want.

Olivier (*stopping him with a gesture*).—One moment! Would
it be civil thus to sit at table without paying your scot and share
of the supper?

Gringoire (*out of countenance*).—Pay? I haven't a red
farthing.

Olivier.—If the Muses dispense but little gold and silver, they
have contrived to lavish other treasures on you. You have
imagination, noble thoughts, the gift of rhyme.

Gringoire (*sadly*).—Such gifts serve no purpose when one
starves, and that is what has happened to me to-day. What
do I say? to-day! Every day.

Olivier.—Understand me. I mean that before satiating
your appetite, you must recite to us one of those odes whose
inspiration the Muses gave you.

Gringoire.—Oh! my lord, my appetite is more hasty than
your ears. (*He starts to approach the table.*)

Olivier (*stopping him*).—Not so. Your verses first. Drink
and eat afterward.

Gringoire.—I assure you that my voice is very ill.

Nicole (*to* GRINGOIRE).—Good courage!

Gringoire (*aside*).—Well, the shortest way is to yield, I see well enough. (*Aloud.*) Will you have me recite some fragment from my poem of the "Folles entreprises?"

Olivier.—No.

Gringoire.—"La Description de Procès et de sa figure?"

Olivier (*interrupting*).—No. A ballad rather. Something that smacks of Gallic soil?

Gringoire (*agreeably surprised*).—Well, that one whose refrain runs: "Car Dieu bénit tous les Miséricords!"

Olivier.—No. Declaim rather that ballad—that one—you know—so popular in the town, so delightful to those to whom it is sung under the breath?

Nicole (*aside*).—Ah! I guess him now!

Gringoire (*uneasily*).—I don't know what you mean.

Nicole (*aside*).—What a wicked man!

Olivier.—Good! Will you say that you don't know the "Ballade des Pendus?"

Gringoire (*checking a start*).—What is that?

Olivier.—The last ballad that you composed.

Gringoire (*much frightened*).—It is not true.

Nicole.—Certainly not.

The King.—Leave them alone, dame Nicole. Listen.

Nicole (*aside, looking at* GRINGOIRE *with pity*).—Ah! The poor fellow! The barber won't leave a crumb of him.

Olivier.—Who nowadays, if not the illustrious poet Gringoire, could compose a ballad like that, whose notes fall so exactly from one couplet to another, like blasts of the horn in the forest?

Gringoire (*flattered*).—It is certain that the rhymes are worked in with tolerable congruity.

Olivier.—Ah! you know it?

Gringoire (*aside*).—My renown betrays me. (*Aloud.*) I should be, I assure you, at a great loss how to recite it. I do not know it.

Olivier.—I thought you, as ourselves, a faithful servant of the sovereign, but having the courage to think aloud, and tell the truth to all, even the King,———

Gringoire (*somewhat shaken*).—Ah! those are your compliments!

Olivier.—But since I have been mistaken, God keep you, Master Gringoire. This is the street door.

Gringoire (regretfully).—What! leave this house and these odours! without having eaten!

Olivier.—It is your desire, you know.

Gringoire.—This is the punishment of Tantalus, who had stolen a golden dog in Crete. I am a hundred times hungrier than a moment ago. (*With despair*) Sirs . . .

Olivier.—Let's say no more about it. Let us part without rancour. (*Pushing him toward the door.*)

Gringoire (in despair).—Yes.

Olivier.—Our poor supper, to be insulted in this way. Admire this goose.

Gringoire.—It makes my mouth water.

Olivier (picking up a dish from the table and showing it to GRINGOIRE).—See what fat and succulent flesh! (*He approaches* GRINGOIRE *and holds a dish for him to smell.*)

Gringoire.—Sweet odour! this gentleman is right. He takes liberties in his thought, but he has a good heart. (*Overcome by hunger.*) Well, since you insist——

Nicole (in terror).—What is he going to do?

Olivier (stopping NICOLE *with glance. Severely.*)—Dame Andry!

Gringoire.—Would you care to hear it too, Madame? Well, since everybody desires it——

The King.—Of course.

Gringoire.—I will recite to you the "Ballade des Pendus." (*To the King, proudly and confidentially.*) It is my own. (*Simply.*) It is an idea that came upon me in crossing the forest of Plessis, where there was many a man dangling from the branches. Perhaps they had been put there for fear that the morning dew might wet their feet!

Nicole (aside).—He will not be still!

The King (to GRINGOIRE).—Well?

Gringoire.—Here it is.

BALLADE DES PENDUS

"Sur ses larges bras étendus,
La forêt où s'éveille Flore,
A des chapelets des pendus
Que le matin caresse et dore.
Ce bois sombre, où le chêne arbore
Des grappes de fruits inouïs
Même chez le Turc et le Moore,
C'est le verger du roi Louis"*

Olivier.—A good beginning!

Nicole (turns to the King in supplication).—Pity!

The King (tranquilly, to GRINGOIRE).—And the rest?

Gringoire.—

> Tous ces pauvres gens morfondus,
> Roulant des pensers qu' on ignore,
> Dans les tourbillons éperdus
> Voltigent, palpitants encore.
> Le soleil levant les dévore.
> Regardez-les, cieux éblouis,
> Danser dans les feux de l'aurore,
> C'est le verger du roi Louis."*

Olivier (repeating ironically the refrain.)

> "Le verger du roi Louis!"

The King (unmoved as before).—Very good.   (*To* GRINGOIRE.)
Continue.

Gringoire.—The third stanza is still more diverting

The King.—Is it possible?

Gringoire.—You shall see.

> "Ces pendus, du diable entendus,
> Appellent des pendus encore.
> Tandis qu' aux cieux, d'azur tendus,
> Où semble luire un météore.
> La rosée en l'air s'évapore,
> Un essaim d'oiseau réjouis
> Par-dessus leur tête picore
> C'est le verger du roi Louis."*

Nicole (aside).—Oh! unhappy man!

(GRINGOIRE *turns around.   All are silent.*)

Gringoire.—Well, what say you to that. (*Aside.*)   They

---

*THE BALLAD OF THE HANGED

On its broad arms swung, the forest where Flora awakes, has chaplets of hanged men that the morning caresses and gilds. This sombre wood, where the oak tree bears clusters of fruits that are strange even to the Turk and Moor. This is the royal orchard of Louis.

All these poor chilly people, thinking thoughts that we know not of, dizzily swing with many a throb, in the sweeping gusts of wind. The rising sun devours them. Watch them, dazzled heavens, dancing in the glow of dawn. This is the royal orchard of Louis.

These hanged by the devil heard call for still more hanged. While to Heaven in azure draped, where a meteor seems to shine, the dew melts away in the air. A swarm of merry birds, pecks away above their heads. This is the royal orchard of Louis.

certainly are not cheerful. Only the old man seems to have been pleased. Doubtless he's a good judge.

The King (*to* GRINGOIRE).—But isn't it customary to have an envoy after the three couplets?

Gringoire.—Yes! I saw at once that you were not of the uninitiated.

The King.—The Envoy should begin, I fancy, with the word *Prince.*

Gringoire.—Oh! that is indispensable, like the eyes of Argus in the peacock's tail. *Prince!* Only, you understand, I know no prince.

The King.—That's provoking!

Gringoire (*with an air of shrewdness*).—I know, however, I might easily offer my ballad to the duke of Brittany or my lord of Normandy.

The King.—To be sure. What hinders you?

Gringoire (*simply*).—Just this, that I am much too fond of France, and even of King Louis—in spite of all! But I am like you. I tell him the truth about himself as well! He who loves well———

The King.—Punishes well. It is right. Let us hear the Envoy.

Gringoire.—

ENVOY

"Prince, il est un bois que décore
Un tas de pendus, enfouis
Dans le doux feuillage sonore.
C'est le verger du roi Louis!"*

Olivier (*to* GRINGOIRE).—Master Gringoire, one cannot polish verses with a more delightfully comic turn.

Gringoire (*modestly*).—Ah! Lord!

The King.—You may appreciate this praise. People agree in praising the taste of Olivier-le-Daim!

Gringoire (*terrified*).—Olivier-de-Diable!

Olivier (*to the King*).—That's a nickname I owe to you, Sire.

Gringoire.—The King!

The King.—Yes, the King!

Gringoire (*overwhelmed*).—The King! I shall *not* sup at all now. (*Stands still in dismay. All are silent.*)

---

*ENVOY
Prince, there is a wood that is garnished with bevies of hanged men, buried in the soft and rustling leaves. This is the royal orchard of Louis.

The King.—You have nothing more to say?

Gringore.—Sire, though I am struck dumb, I think none the less.

The King.—You think perhaps that after having so well sung the hanged——

Gringoire.—Nothing can prevent me——

Olivier.—From being hanged yourself.

Gringoire (choking).—Ah!

Nicole (imploring the King's mercy).—Sire!

(*The King looks at* NICOLE *with an air of understanding.*)

The King (pointing to OLIVIER-LE-DAIM.).—He spoke without my order. But he may have told the truth.

Nicole (whispering to the King).—I saw you smile. The King pardons.

The King (good-humouredly).—I did not say that.

Gringoire.—Hanged! (*Ingenuously to the King.*) Without a supper?

The King (looking at him).—Couldst thou?

Gringoire.—Yes. *I* might very easily. But the King might not.

The King (laughing frankly).—Bah! What a fancy is that. That is attributing to me a spirit of vengeance unworthy of a christian and a gentleman. I do not send my friends to bed fasting. Thou shalt sup.

Gringoire.—At last!

The King.—Eat and drink to thy heart's content,—if thou hast a fancy to!

Gringoire (his face illumined, approaching the table).—To be sure I have!

The King.—Dame Nicole, you have at hand all that is necessary for the best drinking. You will fill his glass.

Nicole.—As for that, yes, poor lamb! (*Aside.*) His good day* has come!

Simon.—He must have plenty of drink at least.

The King.—You, Olivier, will serve our guest.

Gringoire.—Oh! I can help myself.

Olivier (humiliated).—I, Sire!

The King.—You may do so without belittling yourself. I do not forget that I ennobled you. But a lord may serve a poet.

Gringoire (proudly).—Is it so? Well, Sire (*Kneeling*) grant me pardon! I have offended you, but you take my life, I can give you no more!

---

*Conceded to criminals before they were executed.

The King (aside).—Good. (*Motioning* Gringoire *to the table*). Seat thyself and be quick.

Gringoire (rising).—It is right, I have no time to lose, (*He sits at the table and eats,* Olivier-le-Daim *serves him,* Nicole Andry *pours his drink.*) if this feast which I am to enjoy is to be the last I ever shall enjoy! (*The King has seated himself in an arm-chair by* Gringoire's *side and amuses himself by watching him;* Gringoire *eats and drinks with desperate avidity.*) The last, did I say! 'Tis really the first. (*He cuts into an enormous pasty.*) O what a marvellous pasty with its donjons and towers! Will you believe me? Well, that is what I have dreamed of since my entrance into this world. Understand! I have always been hungry. It has been going on for a year, two years, ten years! but in the long run one is always nothing but hungry just the same. Every morning I would say to the rising sun, every evening to the white stars: "So then, to-day is a fast day!" They would answer me, the kindly stars, but they could not give me bread. They had none. (*To* Olivier-le-Daim, *who passes him a dish.*) Many thanks, my lord. (*To the King.*) How easy it must be to be good, when there are such good things to eat! *I* am very good, believe me, I care for the most wretched creatures,——

Nicole (to the King).—Good innocent soul!

Gringoire (continuing).—And yet, that is the first time that I have touched, even with my eyes, such victuals as that. (*To* Nicole Andry, *who pours him a drink.*) Thank you, Madame. Oh! what nice clear wine! Ah! (*He drinks.*) That inspires joy, sunlight and all virtues in your heart. How well I shall live! Who then would have it that I should be hanged? I assure you I do not believe it at all now. (*To the King.*) What good would it do you to hang a nursling of Calliope and the holy Parnassian choir, who, Sire, can recount your exploits to the future race, and make them as durable in the memory of men as those of Amadis of Gaul and the chevalier Perseus?

The King.—Thou hast made such a good beginning!

Gringoire (piteously).—Not very good.

The King.—

"Ces pendus, du diable entendus,
    Appellent des pendus encore."

Gringoire (with an expression of doubt).—Oh! they call them!

Mark you, Sire, good sense is not my strong point. (*Modestly.*) I have naught but genius. Besides, if you hang me, what matter! I am very good to concern myself with it. (*He rises.*) What have I left to do on this planet, now turned cold? I have loved the rose and the glorious lily, I sang like the grasshopper, I played mystery-plays to the glory of the saints, and I see no omission of mine, save leaving some little Gringoires to shiver with hunger and lie on the hard ground. Now frankly, it isn't worth while. The only thing I had neglected until now was to sup. And I have supped well. I had offended the King our lord, I begged his pardon on my knees. My affairs are settled, everything is for the best, and now Master Simon Fourniez, I bless the summer evening when for the first time I passed your house.

Simon.—What summer evening.?

(GRINGOIRE *first rests his elbows on the King's arm-chair, then without noticing what he is doing, seats himself in it.* OLIVIER-LE-DAIM *rushes at him in a fury, but with a glance the King stops the barber, and with a smile signs to him not to molest* GRINGOIRE.)

Gringoire (*giving way to the ecstasy of his revery, and gradually completely forgetting the presence of those about him*).—You see, a hungry poet is much like a giddy-pated moth. The evening I mean (it was the time when the setting sun clothes the sky in rosy red and gold), passing through the Mall du Chardouneret, I saw your window-panes glistening in their leaden settings, filled by the sun with flashing darts of light, and without knowing why I flew to the flame! I approached and through those beautiful blazing panes, I saw the sparkle of ruddy fruits, I saw the glint of plate and the sparkle of silver porringers, I realized that there was to be eating there and I stood in an ecstasy. Suddenly, just above this room, a window opened and a young maid's head appeared, graceful and timorous as the head of Diana, the great nymph with the silent heart, when she breathes deep of the free air of the forest. The golden rays playing about her hair and her rosy brow made her a celestial halo, and I thought at once that she was a saint out of Paradise!

Nicole (*in a whisper to the King*).—It was our Loyse!

Gringoire.—She seemed so honest and so proud! But afterwards I realised that she was only a child, seeing a smile stamped with ineffable kindness flitting in the light of her rosy lips. Then, you may understand, my feet were riveted to the ground, and I could not take my eyes off this house, in which just then were gathered all that I was destined never to possess, a good supper served in rich plate, and a young maid, worthy the adoration of the angels!

The King (whispers to NICOLE).—Well! Nicole, there's a poor dreamer who properly admires my dear god-daughter! what sayst thou to that?

Simon (aside).—A fine treat for my daughter to be stared out of countenance by this phantom, himself as transparent as a pane in a lantern!

Gringoire.—I returned every day, for nothing draws us on more than the deceiving smile of the fancy! But, as the sage has said, everything comes in the end, even those we desire. To-day, at last, I have feasted like Belshazzar, prince of Babylon. But I was shaping another wish, for man is insatiable.

The King (rests his elbows on the chair in which GRINGOIRE *is sitting).*—What is this wish?

Gringoire, noticing his mistake and rising hastily).—That I might once more have seen that fair young girl of the window—

Simon.—No, not that.

Olivier (aside).—Good.

Gringoire (who has not heard SIMON FOURNIEZ, *continuing).*— But I shall see her again, since you send me away before her to await her in Heaven where all the angels are. Well, then, I care for nothing more, and if the moment of your whim has come, I can die gayly and bravely.

The King (aside).—There's a man!

Nicole (aside).—The King does not yet say that he pardons!

The King (in a whisper to NICOLE).—Nicole, tell me: dost thou believe that Loyse—could love this Gringoire?

Nicole.—What!

The King.—Do not be amazed. Could she love him?

Nicole.—Would to Heaven! But——

(*She points to* GRINGOIRE'S *lean face.*)

The King.—I understand thee. (*Aside.*) She is right perhaps. (*After reflection and as if to himself.*) 'Tis all one, in this little world that might fit within the hollow of my hand, I see man and the cords that move him, just as in more illustrious intrigues and it will amuse me to see the story's end.

Olivier.—Sire, may I now lead hence Master Pierre Gringoire?

The King (annoyed by OLIVIER'S *persistency).*—No. Let him stay. I desire to speak with him alone a moment.

Olivier.—Eh! What!

The King (severely).—Did you hear me? Away with you, and do not return until I call you.

Olivier (aside).—The King is foolish when good-humoured. He will do something foolish. But, patience! (*Bows to the* KING *and goes off in a mute rage.*)

The King.—My dear Simon, and you, dame Nicole, leave me alone, I pray you, with Master Pierre Gringoire. I must have a word with him.

Gringoire (aside, while SIMON FOURNIEZ *and* NICOLE ANDRY *take leave of the King and go out)*.—Speak to me! Good Saint Peter my patron saint, what can he want to say to me?

SCENE V

The King.—Pierre Gringoire, I like such men as thou, when they speak well in rhyme and rhythm. I pardon thee.

Gringoire (falling to his knees).—Ah! Sire! "God blesses all the merciful!"

The King.—Yes, I pardon thee. On one condition.

Gringoire.—Do with me what you please.

The King.—I shall find thee a wife.

Gringoire.—Oh! Sire, why not make my pardon complete?

The King.—What! hungry poet! Can it be so pitiable a state to have a good housewife by thy fireside?

Gringoire (rising).—Sire, do you not desire to punish me more cruelly than I deserve? I feel I have no heart to marry some dowager who was a contemporary of Charlemagne.

The King.—She of whom I speak is seventeen this day.

Gringoire.—So then, it is because Heaven has afflicted her with some queer and supernatural ugliness?

The King.—She is as fair as she is young, and very like a blowing rose.

Gringoire (turning pale).—I guess it Sire. But free and spotless under Heaven's arch, I think myself too poor to do without my virtue and good fame.

The King.—Silence! The maid whose husband thou shalt be is pure as ermine, whose sacred whiteness naught should soil.

Gringoire.—In good earnest? (*Seriously.*) But I have no other bed than the green forest and no other cup or bowl than my closed hand: I cannot begin my housekeeping with such poor furniture.

The King.—Take no thought of that. Thou must remember that I am not generous by halves.

Gringoire.—Sire, you are generous as the southern sun! But who is to persuade the maid to be my wife?

The King.—Who? Thyself. Thou shalt look at her as but a moment ago, thou didst look at Master Simon's supper, and thou shalt say to her: "Will you be my wife?"

Gringoire.—I shall never dare.

The King.—Thou must.

Gringoire.—As well propose an accompaniment to the Iliad on a reed-pipe.

The King.—It's only a matter of pleasing.

Gringoire.—Precisely. With this face I have! I feel ugly and poor and when I *have* tried to stammer words of love, they have been so harshly received that I have sentenced myself forever. Mark you, Sire, one day (it was in the forest near by), I saw passing on her spirited steed some young huntress who had strayed far from her retinue. Her face shone with a light divine and she was covered with gold and sapphires. I threw myself before her stretching out my hands to this heroic nymph and cried: "Oh! how fair you are!" She stopped her horse and began to laugh, so loud and long that I feared she might die on the spot. Once more I dared to speak of love to a peasant maid, as poor as I, with hardly more than a few tattered rags to clothe her. *She* was different, looked on me with an air of profound pity, and was so grieved that she could not think me fine, that without saying a word, she shed two great tears. The angels, doubtless, saved them.

The King.—So, thou dost abandon thyself. When I give thee the means of life!

Gringoire.—Fantastic means!

The King.—O cowardice! Rare cowardice of a halting man when he has at his service a stronger weapon than lances and swords! What! thou art a poet, consequently skilful in all the wiles and caresses of language, and the love of life inspires thee not! Know this: while our salvation depends on any living being, and our tongues have not been cut out—nothing is lost. A year ago Gringoire, where was this King who now speaks to thee? Dost thou remember? At Péronne, in the palace of duke Charles, prisoner of a vassal whose interest demanded his destruction, violent, not knowing himself whether he would or would not slay him: those are our experiences in the obscure beginnings of great temptations! Whom did he see about the duke? His own enemies, turncoats all! His jailer persisted in thinking himself offended. For pleasure house, he had a sombre turret in which had flowed the blood of a King of France, slain by a Vermandois! His gold! They thought him so thoroughly ruined that those by whom he sent it to his creatures put it in their pockets. Nothing could win his way out but his agile thoughts; but, thank Heaven, he found opportunity to speak to his enemy, and here he is, the conqueror, feared, master of himself and others, and taking his revenge. And thou Gringoire, thou who hast tasted the sacred honey, whom hast thou to convince? A child, a capricious little girl, a woman, a varying and changing being who can be moulded like soft wax! and thou art fearful!

Gringoire.—Yes.

The King.—And so thou wilt find it easier to die!

Gringoire.—Yes, Sire. For if I speak, as you desire, to this strange young girl, I know well enough what will happen. She will begin to laugh heartily, like the young Diana of the forest of Plessis.

The King.—She will not laugh.

Gringoire.—Then she will weep like the beggar girl. It is one or the other. None love *me* nor shall I love either.

The King.—Thou art not sincere. But I guess thy meaning. Thou dost fear her to whom I shall affiance the hope of thy life. Thou sayest that she cannot love thee, Gringoire? But then, why hast thou kept in thine eyes the living reflection of her angelic beauty? Why is thy heart filled with her? Why did thou desire to see her again but a few moments ago?

Gringoire.—Whom do you mean, Sire?

The King.—She, by Heaven! The maid of the window, whom thou hast loved at sight and whom thou wouldst refuse, Loyse, daughter of Simon Fourniez.

Gringoire (in amaze).—What!

The King.—Well yes, the two are but one. Dost thou fear her still? Wilt thou still die?

Gringoire (almost swooning).—Oh! Sire! do not tell me that it is she, for then I should die at once.

The King (observing Gringoire *curiously).*—I thought thee braver. What will it be when thou dost see her here, presently!

Gringoire.—At the very thought my knees shake and my heart is in my throat!

The King.—Come, come we must make an end of this. (*Goes to the door and calls.*) Ho! friend Simon! Dame Nicole! (*Laughing, to* GRINGOIRE.) My faith, I thought thou would'st fall in a swoon, like a woman!

SCENE VI

Nicole (*entering*).—He has pardoned!

Simon (*bringing* LOYSE *whom the King does not see at first*)—Sire, here we are.

The King (*to* SIMON).—Well, Simon, thy daughter.

Simon (*piteously*).—Sire, I had not the courage to leave her imprisoned in her room. I was foolishly touched, like the old goose I am. (*The King smiles.*) You think me weak, do you not?

The King (*laughing*).—On the contrary. Bring her in.

Gringoire (*aside*).—It is she. (*He leans on a piece of furniture almost ready to swoon.*)

Loyse (*to the King*).—Sire, I am delivered with all the honours of war! (*She embraces* SIMON *who lets her have her way and wipes away a tear.*) The gates of the citadel have been opened to me and I did not surrender my arms.

The King (*gaily*).—Good! But you must still obtain the King's pardon.

Loyse (*laughing*).—Oh! the King, I have no fear of him! (*In a whisper, to the King.*) He is just!

The King.—Thou art right. (*He takes* LOYSE *aside and speaks so as to be heard only by* LOYSE *and* NICOLE.) Tell me (*Pointing to* GRINGOIRE) How do you like that fellow?

Loyse (*looking about her*).—Where do you mean?

The King.—Over there.

Loyse (*after gazing at* GRINGOIRE).—He is not beautiful. He appears sad and humiliated.

Nicole (*whispers to the King*).—Did I not tell you, Sire?

The King (*to* NICOLE).—I shall have it off my mind. I shall find out whether the inner light of the soul cannot sometimes embellish a poor face, and whether the subtle flame of a mind may not suffice to awaken love! (*To* LOYSE.) Pierre Gringoire, my servant, has something to ask of thee in my name. You must grant him a moment's hearing.

Simon.—He— Sire, that starveling speak for you! (*Laughing.*) Ha! ha! ha! what a merry madness!

The King (to SIMON).—Thou mayst well, not so, upon my faith as a gentleman—leave our Loyse alone with him for a few moments?

Simon.—Oh! as for that, Sire, as long as you like! There's no danger in that. Gringoire is a cajoler of girls whom I might very well put out in my orchard, as a scarecrow for the birds!

Gringoire (aside, dolefully).—She hears that!

The King (to LOYSE).—Listen, to this young man, I beg thee. Wilt thou Loyse?

Loyse.—Oh, gladly!

The King.—Good my daughter. (*Seeing the door open.*) But who comes here without my order? Olivier!

SCENE VII

The King (to OLIVIER).—Did I not forbid you, sir, and out of regard for yourself to interrupt at a moment when I intend to decide the future of Loyse?

Olivier (aside).—I come in time. (*Aloud.*) When Your Majesty's interests are at stake, should I not at need, infringe your orders?

The King.—I know these hypocritical pretexts. You must obey and nothing more.

Olivier.—Even when my King's dearest plans are menaced?

The King.—What plans? Speak, sir.

Olivier (pointing to the persons present).—In their presence?

The King.—Before them all! Speak, I tell thee, and woe to thee if thou dost alarm me to no purpose!

Olivier.—Would to Heaven, Sire, that Your Majesty had only to punish the disobedience of his faithful servant. But you will have to punish other crimes more dangerous than that.

The King.—What dost thou mean?

Olivier.—That exchange of Guyenne for Champagne—

The King (trembling, with a gesture motioning LOYSE *away*).— Well, that exchange?

Olivier.—The exchange will not be made.

The King.—What do you say?

Olivier.—My lord your brother refuses.

The King (beside himself).—He refuses!

Olivier.—Did you desire the Duke of Burgundy to be ignorant of your intentions?

The King.—Yes.

Olivier.—He knows them.

The King.—Who is the traitor?

Olivier.—The traitor, Sire, is he who by his letters warned Duke Charles of your plans! I finally succeeded in intercepting one of his letters. Read, Sire! (*Presents him an unfolded letter.*) and Your Majesty may say whether I have done my duty.

The King (*after glancing at the letter*).—La Balue! He, my creature! (*Reading.*) "Believe in all truth My Lord, a discreet servant who is much less the King's man than yours!" Ah! La Balue! to regret this letter that thou hast written, *thou* shalt have a night so long, so dark and so profound, that thou shalt need an effort of the memory to recall the splendour of the sun and the light of day!

Loyse (*unable to hear, but frightened by the King's anger. To SIMON*).—What ails the King? I have never seen him thus.

The King (*rising*).—But what am I saying? Doubtless he has fled!

Olivier.—Not so far that I could not reach him.

The King (*breathing more freely*).—The fool! We have him. I thank thee, Olivier, thou art a good servant, a faithful friend. I shall not forget it. (*With increasing rage.*) Ah! my anger slept and now 'tis waked. So then, this is not the end, master rebels and you need profitable examples: you shall have them! You thought that France was but a blooming garden about your close-locked donjons? No, my masters: France is a forest whose woodsman I am, and I shall lop off every branch in my way, with rope, sword and axe!

Olivier.—My lord de la Balue is a prince of the Church.

The King.—I know it, his life is sacred. I shall not touch La Balue's life. (*Paling with rage.*) But I am saving him a retreat—Come!

Simon (*approaching the King*).—Sire!

The King.—What? What is it? What dost thou desire?

Simon.—The King goes without telling me——

The King.—What have I to tell thee? Have I not wasted time enough in the gossip of thy shop?

Simon (*choking*).—My shop!

The King.—To thy yardstick, good man, to thy yardstick!

Simon (*unconscious of what he says*).—I go, Sire. It is below

Olivier.—But Gringoire——

The King (as in a dream).—Gringoire? What do you mean by Gringoire?

Olivier.—That rebel who jeers at Your Majesty's justice.

The King.—Jeers? Hang him!

Nicole.—Sire, Your Majesty forgets that you have pardoned him.

The King (collecting himself).—It is true. I was wrong. I followed my first impulse, which was worthless. For a just King, indulgence is a crime. Kindness and pardon breed ingrates.

Nicole.—Oh! Sire!

The King (to NICOLE).—Leave me. (*To GRINGOIRE, harshly*). I had laid a condition upon thee for the redemption of thy life.

Nicole.—Suppose he cannot fulfill it!

The King.—So much the better: God does not will that I should pardon. (*To GRINGOIRE*.) However, it is thy concern. In an hour thou shalt have decided thy fate. Princes and lords are not enough? So be it: even in the mire shall I seek rebels to chastise. (NICOLE *offers to speak; the King, with a gesture, imposes silence upon her*.) Enough! Enough! (*Exit*.)

Loyse (to SIMON).—What in the world is the matter, father? What is the matter? (*Watching the King with terror*.) What a change!

Simon (shaking his fist at GRINGOIRE).—To thy yardstick! And it is for that scoundrel that the King has so treated me. A hatless and shoeless beggar!

Olivier.—Master Simon Fourniez, and you dame Nicole Andry, do you retire, and let the demoiselle Loyse (*pointing to* GRINGOIRE) remain alone with this man.

Simon.—That barefoot rascal with my daughter!

Nicole (drawing SIMON away).—The King wills.

Simon (to GRINGOIRE).—Buffoon, mountebank! (*Tearing himself from NICOLE's grasp and turning backward.—Furiously*.) Actor!

Loyse.—Farewell, father. (*Exit SIMON and NICOLE*.)

Olivier (to GRINGOIRE).—In one hour. (*Going to the door, addressing the officer standing outside*.) See to it that your soldiers guard each exit of this house and let no one issue from it under penalty of death. (*He disappears—The door closes behind him*.)

Scene VIII

Gringoire (aside).—Come, Gringoire, that is the simplest thing in the world. Covered, as thou art, with their insults, to win her love! In how long, my good sirs? In an instant, at once! Well and good! they should have said it sooner: it is so easy!

Loyse (aside).—What is the matter? Who is this man. The King wills me to listen to him and at the same time scourges him with his anger. What is he going to ask me? What can I do for him? (*Aloud to* Gringoire.) You have to speak to me?

Gringoire.—I? not at all.

Loyse.—That however is not what the King told me.

Gringore.—Ah! yes, the King has ordered me to put before you a strange and facetious proposal.

Loyse.—Make it then!

Gringoire.—You will refuse.

Loyse.—Tell me, however.

Gringoire.—The King has ordered me to ask you——

Loyse.—What?

Gringoire.—If you would— (*Aside.*) The words will not come.

Loyse.—If I would——

Gringoire.—No, if, I, could—no, I am mistaken! In short, the King—desires to get you a husband.

Loyse.—I know it. The King has already told me. But whom does he command me to marry.

Gringoire.—He leaves you free. You have still the right to refuse. It is the *man* the King proposes who would be obliged to win your love.

Loyse.—But I ask you again, who is this man?

Gringoire.—What difference does it make to you? (*Shrugging his shoulders.*) You cannot love him.

Loyse.—What difference does it make to you also? Come, now, who is he?

Gringoire.—Who and what is he? Oh, I shall explain to you at once. Imagine this. You are dainty and enchanting, he is ugly and sickly. You are rich and well attired, he is poor, hungry and almost naked. You are gay and joyous; and he, when he needs not to rouse the laughter of the passers-by, is melancholy. You see very well that to offer you this wretch, is really to offer the night owl to the meadow lark.

Loyse (*aside, with naive terror*).—Is it he? Oh! no! (*Aloud.*) You are laughing at me. The King loves me; so it is impossible that he has made such a choice for me!

Gringoire.—Really, it is impossible. But it is true, however.

Loyse.—But how can this wretch that you have described to me have attracted the King's attention?

Gringoire.—The King's attention? You say well. He has attracted it to be sure and more than he wanted. How? By making verses.

Loyse (*astonished*).—Verses?

Gringoire.—Yes, lady. An idler's recreation. It consists in fitting together words that fill the ear like an insistent strain of music, in which, one way and another, they paint all things to the life, and among which from time to time are coupled twin sounds, whose accord seems to tinkle playfully, like little golden bells.

Loyse.—What! a sport so frivolous, so puerile, when there are swords, when one may fight! when one may live!

Gringoire.—Yes, one may live! but, what would you have, this dreamer, (and in all ages there has been a man like him) prefers to relate the actions, the loves and deeds of prowess of others in songs in which the false is mingled with the true.

Loyse.—Why, that man is a fool or a coward.

Gringoire (*aside, with a start*).—A coward! (*Aloud, proudly.*) This coward, lady, in days that are far behind us, led armies at his heels, and he gave them the enthusiasm that wins heroic battles! This madman, had a lute that a people of sages and demigods listened to as to a heavenly voice, and they crowned his brow with green laurel!

Loyse.—Ah! of course, among pagan idolaters. But among us to-day!

Gringoire (*sadly*).—To-day? It is different. People think as you do yourself.

Loyse.—But who can have persuaded the King's—protégé to follow such a trade?

Gringoire (*simply*).—No one. The trade followed by this idle singer, this poet (so they called him once), no one advises him to follow. God gives it to him.

Loyse.—God! and why so? Why should he condemn human beings to be useless, and exempt from all duty?

Gringoire.—God has none of this cruel scorn! All have their duty in this world: the poet too! Look you, I shall speak of a thing that perhaps may make you smile, you who are all youth and all grace! for certainly you have never known that bitter torment that consists in suffering the woes of others, in saying to oneself every moment when one feels happiest: "At this very moment when I feel this joy, there are thousands of beings who weep, who groan, who undergo unspeakable torture, who, in their despair, see the lingering death of the objects of their dearest love, and feel a strip torn bleeding from their hearts!" *That* has never happened to you?

Loyse.—You are mistaken. To know that so many beings sob, bow beneath their burdens, succumb, and yet feel myself strong, brave, and yet of no avail, that is what often makes me hate myself. That is why I should like to be a man, to hold the sword, and redeem with my own blood those who have been devoted to unjust misfortune!

Gringoire (uplifted).—So then, you have a heart! Well, will you know? On earth there are, even in the richest lands, thousands of beings who are born in misery and who will die in misery.

Loyse.—Alas!

Gringoire.—There are serfs bound to the soil who owe their lords all the labour of their arms, and who see hunger, fever, sweeping away from their sides, their wan and shivering little ones. There are weavers, cold and wan, who all unconsciously weave their own winding-sheet! Well, what makes the poet is this: all the sorrows of others he suffers; every secret tear and every secret plaint, every unheard sob are fused in his voice and mingled with his song, and once this winged and fluttering song has escaped his heart, neither sword nor torment can arrest its flight; it flies afar off, with untiring wing, forever, in the air and on the lips of men. It enters the castle and palace, it bursts out in the midst of a merry feast, and it says to the princes of earth:—Listen!

"Rois, qui serez jugés à votre tour,
Songez à ceux qui n'ont ni sou ni maille;
Ayez pitié du peuple tout amour,
Bon pour fouiller le sol, bon pour la taille
Et la charrue, et bon pour la bataille.
Les malheureux sont damnés,—c'est ainsi!
Et leur fardeau n'est jamais adouci.

Les moins meurtris n'ont pas le nécessaire.
Le froid, la pluie et le soleil aussi,
Aux pauvres gens tout est peine et misère."*

Loyse (*sadly*).—Ah! God!
Gringoire.—Listen again!

"Le pauvre hère en son triste séjour
Est tout pareil à ses betes qu'on fouaille.
Vendange-t-il, a-t-l chauffé le four
Pour en festin ou pour une èspousaille,
Le seigneur vient, toujours plus endurci.
Sur son vassal, d'épouvante saisi,
Il met sa main comme un aigle sa serre,
Et lui prend tout en disant: "Me voici!"*

Loyse (*falling to her knees with a sob*).—Ah!
Gringoire (*with a mad joy*).—You weep!
Loyse (*exalted*).—"To the poor all is pain and woe."
Gringoire.—Oh! God!
Loyse (*approaching* GRINGOIRE *and regarding him with emotional curiosity.*)—And he who speaks so with a voice so proud, so eloquent, so tenderly indignant, is the protégé of the King! Why then did you think that I could not love him?
Gringoire (*bitterly*).—Why?
Loyse.—And this warrior, so resigned, so bold, who braves all dangers for others needs to be sustained and consoled in his own misery! This man I would know. Who is he?
Gringoire (*on the point of betraying his secret*).—You desire to know him?
Loyse.—Yes, and save him from himself.
Gringoire.—Save him?
Loyse.—You still hesitate.
Gringoire.—Save him from himself—and from the King—
(*Aside.*) Ah! coward! Canst thou think such a scoundrelly

---

*Kings, who will be judged in your turn, think of those who have neither *sou* nor *maille*; have pity on the loving people, good to delve in the soil, good for the tax and the plough, and good for battle too. The wretches are damned—'tis so! And their burden is never lightened. They that suffer the least have not what they need. Cold and rain and the sun as well. To the poor all is pain and woe.

The poor wretch in his sorry hole is like to his beasts that they scourge. Does he harvest or heat his oven for a feast or a wedding, the lord comes forth with his hardening heart. On his vassal, terror-struck, he puts his hand as an eagle his talon, and takes all from him saying "Here I am!"

thought. Borne with her to paradise by the angels, canst thou think of dropping into thy ignominy and dragging her with thee! Die! To be worthy of a happiness that will never come again. Die! To be no less generous than she and save her in turn.

Loyse.—What answer will you have me make the King? This man's name? I have a right to know.

Gringoire (aside).—Why should I, if she has not guessed!

Loyse (aside).—Ah! I hoped that he would name himself!

Gringoire (aside).—Someone comes. (*Seeing* Olivier *enter.*) It is Olivier! It is deliverance! Thanks to Heaven, my rope will really be my own, for I have won it!

Scene IX

Olivier (entering, to Gringoire*).*—The hour has passed.

Gringoire.—So much the better!

Loyse.—So soon!

Olivier.—Let us go then! (*Aside.*) The King would only be sure to have some foolish fit of clemency.

Gringoire.—Farewell, lady. May all the saints keep you!

Loyse.—But your mission has not ended!

Gringoire.—Pardon, my lady. Master Olivier does not like to wait.

Loyse.—And where does he intend to take you then?

Gringoire.—To a festivity at which they cannot do without me!

Loyse (seeing the pages enter preceding the King).—The King! Ah! all will be explained!

(Loyse, Gringoire *and* Olivier-le-Daim *stand on either side of the door. The King enters without seeing them. He is rubbing his hands and his face wears a joyous expression. He crosses the stage and drops into a great arm-chair to the left.*)

The King.—If there is on earth one complete and unmixed joy, if there is one pleasure that is really divine, it is that of punishing a traitor. Above all when the treason has come to naught and can no longer harm us. Ah! now I feel well. There was no danger—on the contrary—and I am still master of events. (*Perceiving* Olivier-le-Daim). Thou here, my brave and faithful servant? What art thou doing?

Olivier.—Sire, I was carrying out your orders.

The King.—My orders? (*Perceives* Gringoire *and remembers all.*) Gringoire? (*Remembering.*) Ah! one moment!

Olivier.—But——

The King (without listening to him).—Thou hast served me well, Olivier. I shall be grateful to thee.

Olivier.—Sire, Your Majesty already rewards me in deigning to approve my zeal.

The King.—We shall do better still. (*Dismissing him with a gesture.*) Go, Olivier, let me arrange things. Thou shalt lose nothing by it.

Olivier (bowing).—Sire, there is every advantage in relying on you. (*Exit.*)

The King (to himself).—The captaincy of the bridge of Meulan and I shall be quits with him. (*Perceiving* LOYSE.) Loyse! There thou art, my dear! Why stand there? Do I frighten thee?

Loyse.—A little. You have been so cross!

The King (as if waking from a dream).—Cross? Ah! yes. Let us say no more of that. The sight of thee refreshes me. Come. (*He kisses* LOYSE *on the brow.*) But I do not see thy father.

(*A moment or so before* SIMON *and* NICOLE *have entered by the door to the left. They stop a moment at the rear of the stage, looking curiously at the King.*)

Loyse.—He is hiding from you. You treated him so well!

The King.—I! What could I have said to that good, dear friend?

Loyse (pointing to SIMON).*—There he stands yonder, not daring to come forward.

The King (to SIMON).*—Why then? come near, come near, friend Fourniez. Where wert thou then?

Simon.—Where was I? (*Bitterly.*) With my yardstick.

The King.—With thy—(*Smiling*) Good Simon, have I hurt thee? Thy hand! I hold no ill-will against thee. I pardon thee.

Nicole (coming forward).—'Tis very kind. Your Majesty has deigned to treat my brother so ill, that you should hold no grudge against him.

The King.—Nicole! I was wrong to be absent-minded in the presence of a witty woman. Come here, my friends, to my side. Thou too, Gringoire. There is something we must settle, here in this family circle of ours. (*To* GRINGOIRE.) Well, my master, I hope thou hast succeeded in winning thy happiness!

Yes, I am sure that my god-daughter must have appreciated the man that I offered her.

Simon.—What man?

The King.—Is it not so, Loyse?

Loyse (*slyly feigning absent-mindedness*).—What do you mean, Sire? Of whom are you speaking?

The King.—Of the husband I have chosen thee.

Simon.—What husband?

The King.—Dost thou accept?

Loyse.—No.

The King (*amazed*).—No!

Loyse (*aside*).—This time, he will have to speak.

The King.—Thou refusest! Thou, Loyse!

Loyse (*slyly watching* Gringoire).—I cannot marry a stranger—whose very name they wouldn't even tell me!

Nicole (*to the King*).—Ah! I was sure of it! He was brave to the end.

Loyse.—I knew well enough that he was in danger!

The King (*to* Loyse).—Gringoire did not tell thee that he had offended the King his Lord by composing a certain—"Ballade des Pendus," and that to redeem his life—

Loyse (*guessing*).—In one hour, in one moment, he was to—

Gringoire.—Win thy love!

Loyse (*uttering a great cry of joy*).—Ah! (*Advancing to* Gringoire *whom she takes by the hand.*) Sire, this morning I demanded of you a husband capable of heroic deeds, a brave man with hands unstained by spilled blood: Well! there he is, Sire. Give him to me. I love him. I demand the fulfilment of your promise, and I shall be proud to be his companion forever, in life and death!

The King (*to* Simon Fourniez).—Well, Simon?

Simon.—I understand, Sire. You wish my consent?

The King.—Wilt thou give it?

Simon.—You know, Sire, we are not accustomed to refuse each other anything.

The King (*laughing*).—Thank you, friend. (*To* Gringoire.) And thou, Gringoire, what hast thou to say?

Gringoire (*beside himself with joy*).—Sire! She does not laugh!

The King (*gaily*).—Nor does she weep either! (*Whispers to* Gringoire.) Must I tell her now the reason thou hadst for being so timid?

Gringoire (sadly indicating his poor face).—What is the good, Sire, if she does not perceive it?

The King (to SIMON).—My dear ambassador——

Simon (radiant with joy).—Ambassador!

The King.—Now thy daughter is provided for; prepare thyself to start for Flanders. (*Taking* NICOLE *and* LOYSE *by the arm.*) Art thou satisfied with me, Nicole?

Nicole.—Yes my Lord. You are a true King since you can pardon. And what is there sweeter? A man hanged can be useful to no living soul—

Loyse.—While a wood bird or a singing poet is good at least to announce that dawn is breaking and that spring is coming!

CURTAIN FALL.

THE PATH OF THE RUSSIAN THEATRE AND "LE COQ D'OR"

By Alexander Bakshy

GREATLY bewildered, though obviously pleased, the English public has been watching for the last few years the display of wonderful theatrical wares which the fascinating Russian dancers and singers have chosen to bring over to this country. Not only has the spectacle been a startling revelation of the wealth of artistic treasures possessed by that land of snow and vodka and downtrodden "moujicks," but the wares themselves have been dazzling with colours that seemed to overshadow everything of the kind produced at home. First came the ballet, with its feast of gorgeous scenery and transporting dancing, and the public abandoned itself to its Baksts, its Fokins, its Pavlovas and its Karsavinas. Next the opera came, and the melodies of Moussorgsky, Rimsky-Korsakov and Borodin and Chaliapin's most remarkable impersonations captured another corner in the public mind, previously so completely occupied by the Germans and Italians. The season which has just ended has provided the latest wonder: a kind of a cross between ballet and opera which has resulted in the striking production of "Le Coq d'Or." Finally we are promised a season of Russian drama as produced by the famous Moscow Art Theatre, and one can safely predict that it will meet with the same unreserved admiration which has been so generously bestowed upon its other Russian precursors on the English stage.

Admiring however as it does all these various manifestations of the newly discovered Russian Art, the English public seems to be completely in the dark as to their mutual interdependence, their inner significance and the bearing they have on the development of the Theatre, which nowadays everybody professes to take so closely to heart. Taken separately, as isolated phenomena, the Russian productions that have passed before the eyes of the London audiences have betrayed no signs of their origin: of the history of the various movements in Russia appertaining to the theatre, their defeats and victories and the great research and experimental work of which these productions have been the copingstone. "Le Coq d'Or" is perhaps the most significant of them all, being the latest indication of the new principles which are now gradually gaining ground in the Russian theatre. It would, for this reason, be interesting to follow from whence this production has come, and whither it leads.

For the starting point of the modern theatrical movement in Russia one must go back to the end of the 'nineties when the Moscow Art Theatre was born at the initiative of the genius of M. Stanislavsky.

The essential feature of the new theatre was embodied in its peculiar name—"The Moscow *Art* Theatre." Why an "Art" theatre? one may ask. One does not hear of "art painting" or "art music." Music or painting can be good or bad, but "art music"—! The words seem redundant.

Yet there was sense in the appellation of the Moscow Theatre. The end of the last century found the Russian theatre drifting into a state of provincial commonness with slovenliness and vulgarity of detail, pretending to be realistic, flourishing side by side with an exhibition of real dramatic genius evinced by a few gifted actors of the old temperamental school. The backslidings were so obnoxious to the taste of the better educated and more cultured members of the public, that a thorough reform of the theatre seemed to brook no delay. The way of reforming it for the moment was quite clear: the inconsistencies of the scenery were to be vigorously eradicated, and the choice of plays was to agree with the higher intellectual demands of the "intelligentia." As will be seen, in this respect the Moscow Art Theatre was pursuing the same object as the Repertory movement in England. The merit of the first lies in the thoroughness of its methods and the peculiar course it has adopted in carrying them out. The application of "art" principles to the inconsistencies of the scenery resulted in the substitution of the naturalistic imitations (if not the real things themselves) for the badly painted and conventional canvasses of the traditional theatre. The greater discrimination in the choice of plays brought to the stage the chief representatives of the modern drama, Tchekhov foremost amongst them, and with them the whole host of problems that characterize the world of the modern intellectuals.

These two essential factors, the naturalistic method of staging and the allegiance to the intellectual play, have ever since been determining the development of the Moscow Art Theatre. Their joint course, however, has not been running very smoothly. The second factor contained elements that have been for the Theatre a source both of its strength and its weakness. If we look closely into the meaning of the naturalistic method (of which natural scenery and acting are of course essential components) we can easily see that it aims at establishing on the stage an objective world existing independently of and externally to the audience. But to realize any world objectively and at the same time externally is possible only in the terms of the natural phenomena which surround us in our daily life. Thus, however unreal the plot of a play may be, if we wish to give it a semblance of independent existence we are bound to materialise its ideal scenery and to substitute human psychology for its vague spiritualism.

And such has been the method of the Moscow Art Theatre. Whatever the world pictured in the play, the sole ambition of the Theatre has been to make it appear as something objectively given and independent of the audience. Tchekhov in his plays portrayed the world of soft and subtle emotions, in which his heroes appeared to move weak-willed and powerless, reflecting every impulse that came from any close source of disturbance. And the Art Theatre's method of producing Tchekhov's plays has been to create a semblance of a real world in which life is an all pervading stream of gentle emotions. It must be admitted that in these productions the Art Theatre has often been most successful, though not infrequently it has been guilty of attempting to materialize things which were naturally opposed to such a process. But its failure has been made more manifest in its productions of Maeterlinck and Ibsen. There is an atmosphere about the plays by these authors which absolutely defies any attempt of materialization on the stage. The only place where it can be fully realized is in the imagination of the audience, but to achieve this result one must resort to other methods than those employed by the Art Theatre.

The first amongst the Russian stage-managers to recognize the fact was M. Meyerhold who started as a collaborator of M. Stanislavsky, but soon parted ways with him, having come to the conclusion that naturalistic methods are inartistic in themselves and utterly unsuitable for production of symbolical or more or less abstract plays.

During one year of his association with the late Vera Kommissarjevskaia, the famous Russian actress, M. Meyerhold created a new school of the theatre, based on the principles which have since received the name of "stylisme" and "conventionalism." These names, however, though appropriate in themselves, fail to indicate the fundamental difference which distinguished the new movement from the Moscow Art Theatre. This was not so much an opposition between realism and conventionalism as that between the objective attitude towards a performance and the subjective one. The Art Theatre placed the centre of gravity of the production on the stage, M. Meyerhold transferred it to the audience. It would have scarcely made an atom of difference to the self-sufficiency and completeness of the Art Theatre's performance if the audience were to be entirely removed. On the other hand the very life would have been taken out of M. Meyerhold's productions if this experiment were applied to them.

Having, so to speak, taken sides with the audience, M. Meyerhold could not help' rejecting the naturalistic methods. It was no longer a question of picking and choosing whatever one liked out of a complete reproduction of the world on the stage, but rather of evoking a fuller vision of the world by showing a glimpse of it on the boards. It was this subjective vision held by the audience, to which the stage production had to appeal and with which it was indissolubly bound up. And thus the ideas of "stylisme" and "conventionalism" were born to life.

There is a good deal of misconception prevalent with regard to the inner significance of these terms. They were coined to denote something departing from the methods of the realistic school which were supposed to give the only adequate expression of real life. But as was indicated above, all forms of the theatre, as well as of art in general, derive their significance from the attitude taken up by the spectator. So far as "stylisme" and "conventionalism" are concerned they are not more conventional, in the strict sense of the word, than realism itself. The Russian name for "conventionalism" is "conditionalism," and in this form it at once reveals its real nature. This may be expressed in a few words: "certain premises admitted, corresponding conclusions must needs be drawn." If one agrees to assign certain powers to various cards, or chess figures, or mathematical symbols, or government officials, the combinations which may arise in the course of play or calculation or political strife would be neither arbitrary, nor unreal—they would be merely "conditional." In the same way if one attempts to view the world from some peculiar standpoint according to the sentiment or attitude of mind, that dominates one at the moment, or is one's individual peculiarity or national characteristic, the vision of the world one obtains is as real and inevitable in its logic as, say, the indisputable fact that the sky looks dark after the sun has set.

In other words "conventionalism" means an admission of legitimacy of various other standpoints besides the objectively external or realistic one. And "stylisme" gives expression to this admission by subjecting all the sentiments embodied in a work of art to the control of one principal sentiment chosen.

This method accepted, the success of a production will depend on the sensitiveness shown by the producer in discovering the leading sentiment of the play and his cleverness in finding appropriate forms for the expression of this sentiment. The task is by no means an easy one as has unfortunately too often been proved by many who have ventured to tackle it before they have acquired the necessary qualifications. M. Meyerhold himself has been perhaps one of the most successful regisseurs in productions of this kind. The same way be said of M. Fokin, who has applied M. Meyerhold's methods to the domain of the ballet. There is however a difference between the two men. M. Meyerhold has inclined to mystical experiences, as has been shown by his partiality to Maeterlinck. The disposition of M. Fokin on the contrary has been more towards the elementary emotions of passion and love, only refracted through a prism of exotic exuberance and sensuality. Another point of difference between the two is that whilst M. Meyerhold, the originator of the school, has long ago modified his views to such an extent as to form an entirely new conception of the theatre, M. Fokin is still following the method of "style," though in the application of it to his productions he never fails to impress one by the magnificence of staging *the originality* of his conceptions and the supreme mastery of all the subtleties of that radiant and elusive medium—the human body.

It has been left, however, to M. Alexander Benois, the eminent painter and historian of art, who has often declared himself as an opponent of M. Meyerhold's latest theories, to lead the way in the introduction of the new principles into the domain of ballet. To his genius the amazing production of "Le Coq d'Or" owes its origin, marking a change in the history of ballet that is frought with consequences of tremendous magnitude and importance. It is to be hoped that other productions will further develop the features that are only tentatively indicated in this, the first experiment.

However, to understand the latter, one must again revert to the productions of M. Meyerhold. As was pointed out before, the one or another glimpse of the world (the "style") to be revealed on the stage has to find for itself a special form of expression. What forms are there at the command of the play-producer? There was no exhaustive answer to this question at the time when M. Meyerhold entered upon his research work. To gain any knowledge was possible only by experimenting, and this M. Meyerhold actually did. He produced a number of plays by Maeterlinck and found that the best form for expressing their intense religious feeling was to stage them in one plane with the actors playing close to the footlights against flat decorative scenery. The effect aimed at by such staging was to dematerialize the stage and to merge the action of the play in the sway of emotions of the audience. It was soon however discovered that the stage possesses certain properties which are by their very nature opposed to their being tampered with in any arbitrary way. Thus the attempt to create on the stage a space of two dimensions proved inwardly contradictory, since the principal element, the actor, is a being of three dimensions. Further, the pictorial appeal of the decorative scenery seemed to have an adverse effect on the unity of impression, detracting the attention of the audience from the acting. These and further observations led M. Meyerhold to the conviction that the peculiarities of the stage must frankly and unreservedly be admitted and that the only honest way of using the medium of the theatre is never to try to disguise the fact that it is a theatre. Thus the representation of life, realistic or conventional, has been subjected to a higher principle—of the "style" of the theatre—and "theatricality" has become the motto of the new movement. The evolution of the idea has not stopped at this. Its further development led to the recognition of the actor's personal dexterity, of the "mask" and the "grotesque" so characteristic of the Medieval Booth and the seventeenth century's Italian "Commedia dell'Arte," as the fundamental forms of the art of the Theatre. In a number of M. Meyerhold's productions in the Imperial and private theatres in St. Petersburg these principles have been put to the test and proved a source of vital power that has infused fresh blood into the life of the Russian theatre.

We have now arrived at the point at which it will be possible to see in what relation "Le Coq d'Or" stands to these developments. The peculiar feature of the production—the division of parts between the singers and dancers—is an obvious application of the principle of "theatricality." The producer made no attempt to disguise the fact that it was an artificial device specially put up to enhance the scenic effect of the action. The expedient had nothing to do with the demands of realism or of the style of the plot. It was purely and frankly theatrical.

The question arises: How far has it been successful? The producer has been of course bound up by the form of the opera, but taking the production as it has been given, it is easy to find its shortcomings. In the first place, the chorus openly placed on the stage with the evident object of acting as chorus, during the performance soon lost its independent position, as the audience quickly learnt to overlook the discrepancy and to regard the dancers as the actual singers. If this was the desired effect then the whole arrangement, as everything sham, militates against good taste. It would be more appropriate in this case to regard the singers as a part of the orchestra and to treat them as the latter is treated, i. e., hiding them from the audience so that the singing should appear as a mere accompaniment to the movements of the dancers. If on the contrary, as was alleged above, the singers were brought on the stage to act separately and independently the experiment has not been carried on to its logical conclusion. Having come near to the fundamental problem of the chorus and proscenium as connecting links between the stage and the audience, in which form it dominated the Ancient theatre, the producer of "Le Coq d'Or" has not ventured to face it or endeavored to find an appropriate solution. Instead he has preferred to go only half way—satisfied with the extent of originality already achieved and with the indisputable quaintness and poignancy of its effect, enhanced, as it has been, by the conscious use of grotesque scenery and acting. However, the boldness of the experiment, and the vistas of new theatrical forms it opens up before the public, greatly overbalance its shortcomings and fill one with confidence that further progress along the lines of the theatre-platform will not be long delayed.

AN INCIDENT

By Leonid Andreyev

Translated from the Russian by Leo Pasvolsky

Two persons take part in the action: a merchant, KRASNO-
BRUHOV, *who confesses his crime, and a police official. There
is also a policeman,* GAVRILENKO, *who brings in the repenting mer-
chant, and some other living automata who carry him out.*

*The room resembles an unfurnished factory. The official
barks abruptly into the telephone; his voice expresses anger and
astonishment.* GAVRILENKO *leads in the merchant, holding him
respectfully, with two fingers only.* KRASNOBRUHOV *is a fat,
healthy-looking old man, with a red beard. Appears to be very
much excited. He wears no hat, and his clothes are in suspicious
disorder.*

The Official (at the telephone).—Who? What? Why, of
course, I can hear you if I am speaking to you. . . the
murdered? Oh, yes! Yes, yes, two of them. . . Of course
I can hear you. What is it? What *are* the motives? Well?
I can't understand a thing. Who ran away? The wounded man
ran away? Say, what are you talking about? Where did the
wounded man run to?

Gavrilenko.—Your Honor, so I brought him. . .

The Official.—Don't bother me! Oh, yes, so one ran away,
and you're bringing over the other . . . and what about
the murderers? What? Ran away also? Look here, don't
you try to get me all muddled up with those motives of yours!
What's that? I can't make out a blessed thing. Listen to me!
If you want to make the report—Do you hear me?—Go ahead
and make it! Don't whistle through your nose at me. I'm not
a clarinet. What? What music? No, no, I say, I'm not a clarinet.
Do you hear? Hello! Oh, damn you! Hello! (*Hangs up the
receiver, throwing an angry side-glance at* KRASNOBRUHOV. *Then
sits down.*)

The Official.—Well? What do you want?

Gavrilenko.—So, your Honor, if you will permit me to report,

171

he blocked the traffic and the wagons. He came out in the middle of the market place, right in the middle of the traffic and hollered out that he was a merchant and had killed a man, and so I took him along. . . .

The Official.—Drunk? You old goat, drunk as a pig?

Gavrilenko.—Not at all, your Honor, quite sober. Only he stopped in the middle of the market place, right in the road and started hollering out, so that, your Honor, not a wagon could pass, and a big crowd collected. He hollered out 'I killed a human being, brethren, I confess!' And so I brought him over. It's his conscience, your Honor.

The Official.—Why didn't you say that at the beginning, you blockhead! Let him go, Gavrilenko, don't hold him like a dog. Who are you?

Krasnobruhov.—Prokofi Karpovich Krasnobruhov, a merchant. (*Kneels down and says in a repentant tone.*) I confess, brethren! Take me, bind me! I killed a human being!

The Official (*rising to his feet*).—Oh! So that's what you are!

Krasnobruhov.—I confess, brethren, I confess! Let me atone for my sins! I can't stand it any longer! Take me, bind me—I killed a human being! I'm an unconfessed scoundrel, a criminal against nature! I killed a human being! (*Lowers his head to the ground.*)

Gavrilenko.—That's the way he was hollering out there, your Honor, right in the middle of the traffic. . .

The Official.—Shut up! Stand up, now! Tell me all about it. Whom did you kill?

Krasnobruhov (*getting up heavily and smiting himself on the chest*).—I murdered a human being. I want to atone for my crime. I can't stand it any more. It's too much for me. My conscience won't let me live, brethren. Come on, shave me![1]

The Official.—Shave you!

Krasnobruhov.—Shave my head, put me in irons! I want to atone for my crime. (*Sobs aloud.*) I killed a human being. Forgive me, brethren!. (*Falls on his knees again and bows to the ground.*)

The Official.—Up with you! Now talk like a sane man, will you?

Gavrilenko.—That's just the way he did up there, your Honor, and started hollering. . .

[1] In Russia, half of the head of a convict is shaved just before he is deported to Siberia.—Translator's Note.

The Official.—Shut up! What's your name? Is this your trunk?

Krasnobruhov (gets up again and wipes his tears and perspiration).—What trunk? I don't know about any trunk. We deal in vegetables. Oh, Lord! In vegetables. . . .

The Official.—What trunk! Don't know anything about the trunk, hey? But when you stuffed him into the trunk, you knew all about it, eh? And when you shipped his body by freight, you knew it, eh?

Krasnobruhov.—I don't know about any trunks. Wish I could get a drink of water. (*To* GAVRILENKO.) Give me a drink of water, boy, I'm all hoarse. (*Sighs heavily.*) O—oh.

The Official (to GAVRILENKO).—Stay where you are. And you don't know which trunk it is? Gavrilenko, how many trunks have we here?

Gavrilenko.—Four trunks, your Honor, and one suit-case. We've opened three, your Honor, and haven't had time for the fourth yet.

The Official (to the merchant).—Did you hear that?

The Merchant (sighing).—I don't know about any trunks.

The Official.—Where is yours then?

The Merchant.—My what?

The Official.—How should I know whom you killed there, or cut, or strangled? Where's the body?

The Merchant.—The body? Oh, I guess its all rotted away now. (*Falls on his knees again.*) I confess, brethren, I killed a human being! And buried the body, brethren. I thought I could deceive the people, but I see now that I can't do it. My conscience won't let me. I can't sleep or rest at all now. Everything's dark before my eyes and all I have now is my suffering. I want to atone for my sins. Strike me, beat me!

The Official.—Up with you! Speak plainly now!

The Merchant (gets up and mops his face).—I am speaking plain enough, I reckon. I thought that after some time I'd forget it, perhaps, and find joy in life and burn candles to the poor soul. But no! My torment is unnatural. I haven't a minute of rest. And every year it gets worse and worse. I thought it might pass away. And now I confess, brethren! I was sorry for the property. We deal in vegetables and I was ashamed for my wife and children. How could it happen so suddenly? I was a good man all the time, and then, a scoundrel, a murderer, a criminal against nature!

The Official.—Speak to the point, I tell you!

The Merchant.—But I am speaking to the point. Every night I cry and cry. And my wife says to me, says she, 'What's the use of crying here, Karpich, and shedding tears on the pillows? Better go to the people and bow down to the ground and accept the suffering. What difference does it make to you?' says she. 'You're pretty old already; let them send you to Siberia, you can live there, too. And we'll pray for you here. Go on, Karpich, go on!' So we cried together, and cried, and couldn't decide it. It's hard, it's frightful, brethren! When I look around me. . . . We deal in vegetables; you know, carrots, and cabbages and onions. . . (*Sobs.*) And she says to me, 'Go on, Karpich, don't be afraid. Drink some tea, have a little fun, and then go and bear your cross!'—And I tried doing it once. She gave me a clean shirt, and treated me to tea with honey, and combed my hair with her white hand,—but I couldn't do it! I was too weak! Lost my courage! I got as far as the market place and came out into the middle of the street, and suddenly a car came up . . . So I turned into a saloon. I confess, my friends, instead of repentance, I spent three days and three nights in the saloon, polishing the bar and licking the floor. I don't know where all that drink went to. That's what conscience does to you!

The Official.—Yes. That's conscience for you, all right! But I'm very glad, very glad. . . . Gavrilenko, did you hear?

Gavrilenko.—That's just the way he was hollering there, your Honor.

The Official.—Shut up! But go ahead, my friend.

The Merchant.—I'm no friend, I'm an enemy of mankind, a criminal against nature. Take me, bind me! I killed a human being! I'm a murderer! Come now, bind me! Shave me!

The Official.—Yes, yes, I'm very glad to see you repenting. Gavrilenko, do you happen to remember this case? What cases have we?

Gavrilenko.—Don't remember, your Honor!

The Merchant.—Bind me!

The Official.—Yes, yes, I can understand your noble impatience, but . . . And when did it happen? Of course, we know everything, but there are so many cases, you know! Look how many trunks we have. It's like a freight station . . . Whom did you . . . when was it?

The Merchant.—When? Oh, I guess it must be about

twenty-one years. Twenty-one and a little extra may be. About twenty-two, you might say.

The Official.—Twenty-two? What do you want then?

The Merchant.—I thought I'd get over it. But no! It gets worse and worse every year, more and more bitter every day. In the beginning I didn't have any visions, at least. And now visions come to me. I confess, brethren, I'm a murderer!

The Official.—But, but allow me . . . Twenty-two years . . . What guild[2] do you belong to?

The Merchant.—The first. We sell wholesale.

The Official.—Yes, yes, Gavrilenko, a chair. Take a seat, please.

The Merchant.—Wish I could get a drink, I'm all hoarse.

The Official.—And so you had tea with honey again?

The Merchant.—Yes, of course.

The Official.—Gavrilenko, two glasses of tea—make one weak . . . You take your tea weak, don't you? Your name, please?

The Merchant.—Prokofi Karpovich Krasnobruhov. But when are you going to bind me, your Honor?

The Official.—Take a seat, please. And, Prokofi Karpich, isn't that your store on the corner? A wonderful sign you have there! That's real art. You know, sometimes, I am astonished at the artistic beauty of our signs. Why, sometimes my friends ask me, why I don't go to art-galleries, the Hermitage, and so on, you know . . . And I say, 'Why should I go there? Why, my whole district is an art-gallery.' Ye-es! (GAVRILENKO *returns with the tea.*) I'm sorry, but we have no honey here. The office, you know.

The Merchant.—I'm not thinking about honey now. I left the business to my children. Let them have it now. But when are you going to bind me, your Honor? I wish you'd hurry it up.

The Official.—Bind you? Gavrilenko, get out of here! And next time you see a dignified person on the market place, treat him with more respect, do you hear? Where is his hat?

Gavrilenko.—It was lost there in the street. The people left nothing of it. So, your Honor, when he came out there, hollering and . . .

The Official.—Get out! Yes, there's people for you. How

[2] Russian merchants belong to one of three "guilds" according to the size of their business. The first is the highest and requires the largest license-money.—Translator's Note.

can you ever make them understand the fundamentals of law and order, so to speak? I'm sick and tired of them. My friends sometimes ask me, 'How is it, Pavel Petrovich, that we never hear a pleasant word from you?' And how can you expect anything like that? I'd be glad myself, you know, I'm just dying for society conversation. There are so many things in the world, you know! The war, the Cross of St. Sophia, and,—in general,—politics, you know!

The Merchant.—I wish you'd bind me now.

The Official.—Bind you? Why, that's a pure misunderstanding, Prokofi Karpich, a pure misunderstanding. But why don't you drink your tea? Your worthy feelings do you honor and, in general, I'm very glad but—the time limitation. You must have forgotten about the limitation! I hope it wasn't your parents.

The Merchant.—Oh, no, no, not my parents. It was a girl . . . in the woods . . . and I buried her there.

The Official.—Now you see! I understood right away that it wasn't your parents. That's not the kind of man you are! Of course, if it were your parents, you know, well, your father or mother, then there's no time limitation. But for your girl, and in criminal cases generally, murders and so on, everything is covered by the ten years' limitation. So you didn't know that? Is that so? Of course, we'll have to make an investigation, a confirmation, but that's nothing. You shouldn't have excited yourself so. Go back home and sell your vegetables, and we'll be your customers. . . What about the tea, though?

The Merchant.—How can I think about the tea, when I feel as if there were hot coals under me?

The Official.—You shouldn't have tormented yourself so, no indeed! Of course, you weren't acquainted with the Law. You should have gone to a lawyer, instead of to your wife . . .

The Merchant (falls on his knees).—Bind me! Don't make me suffer!

The Official.—Well, now, now, please get up! Why, we can't bind you. You're a queer fellow! Why, if we were to bind every one like you, we shouldn't have enough rope to go round! Go home now and . . We have your address . . .

The Merchant.—But where shall I go to? I've come here. Why don't you bind me, instead of saying that? There is no rope, you say. What's the use of mocking me? I came to you in earnest and you make fun of me! . . . (*sighing*) But, of course, I deserve it. I repent. Bind me! Beat me! Mock me, brethren! Strike this old face of mine; don't spare my beard! I'm a murderer! (*Falls down on his knees.*)

The Official (*impatiently*).—But look here, that's too much! Get up! I'm telling you to go home; I've no time to waste with you. Go home!

The Merchant (*without rising*).—I've no home, brethren, no asylum except the prison! Bind me. (*Shouting*) Shave me!

The Official (*also shouting*).—What do you take me for? A barber? Get up!

The Merchant.—I won't get up! I'm repenting before you and you can't refuse me! My conscience torments me! I don't want your tea. Bind me! Tie my hands! Shave me!

The Official (*calling*).—Gavrilenko! (*The policeman enters.*) Just listen to the way he shouts here! With that conscience of his, eh? As if I had time to bother with you . . . Gavrilenko, raise him!

(GAVRILENKO *attempts to raise the merchant, who resists him.*)

Gavrilenko (*muttering*).—That's just the way he was hollering . . . I can't raise him, your Honor, he won't get up.

The Official.—Ah, he won't? Petruchenko! Sidorenko! Youshchenko! Raise him!

(*The policemen run in, and the four raise the merchant, while the official becomes even more angry.*)

The Official.—Just listen to this! He goes to the very market place and blocks the traffic! Just wait, I'll teach you to block the traffic; I'll teach you to shout in a public place!

The Merchant.—You don't dare! Bind me, or I'll send in a complaint. I don't care! I'll go to the minister himself! I killed a human being! My conscience won't let me live! I repent!

The Official.—Your conscience? My goodness, he's happy about it! And where was your conscience before this? Why didn't you come sooner? Now you are ready enough to go into the market place and create a disorder! Why didn't you come sooner?

The Merchant.—Because I hadn't suffered enough before. And now I can't stand it any more; that's why I came! You daren't refuse me!

The Official.—Hadn't suffered enough? Listen to that mockery. Here we are looking and searching for them, we've got five trunks here and a special bloodhound, and he . . .

He hid himself, the rascal, and not a sound. As though he weren't there. And then he gets out into the market place and starts shouting 'My conscience. Bind me!' Here we are, breaking our heads over the new cases and he comes around with that girl of his . . . Get out! Get out of here!

The Merchant.—I won't go. You daren't drive me back! I've already said good-by to my wife. I won't go!

The Official.—Then you'll say 'Good-morning' to your wife again. My goodness, he said 'Good-by' to his wife, and drank some tea with honey, and put a clean shirt on! I'll bet you had to pour twenty glasses down your throat, before you filled up. And now he comes around here! Get out!

Krasnobruhov.—And did you see me drink it? Maybe only half of it was tea and the other half my bitter tears! I won't go! Send me to Siberia! Put me in irons! Shave my head!

The Official.—There's no prison for you. Go and hire a room in Siberia, if you want to. We've got no prison for you.

The Merchant.—You'll send me to prison! I won't go anywhere else, do you hear me? Brethren, I want to suffer for my deed; I want to go to Siberia for twenty years. I'm a murderer. I killed a human being.

The Official.—No Siberia for you, do you hear? Why didn't you come sooner? We can't send you to prison now. We haven't room enough for real ones. And he comes around here with his conscience! He suffers, the scoundrel! Go ahead and suffer. There is no prison for you.

The Merchant.—So you won't send me . . ?

The Official.—No!

The Merchant.—You'll shave my head, all right.

The Official.—Go and shave yourself!

The Merchant.—No! You shave me. (*Attempts to kneel down; bends his legs at the knees, but is held in the air by the four policemen.*) Brethren, have pity on me! Bind me! Haven't you got a piece of cord somewhere? Any old piece. I won't run away even if you tie me with a piece of twine. My conscience won't let me. Any old piece. Isn't there any room for me at all in prison, your Honor? I don't need much room, your Honor. Please bind me and shave off my gray hair! Please let me walk at least over the edge of the Vladimir[3] trail and get

---

[3]The trail through Russia and western Siberia, over which gangs of convicts are led into the penal colonies.—Translator's Note.

covered with its dust! Give me the shameful badge[4] Cain's badge! Lead me to the hangman, let him torture me!

The Official.—Gavrilenko! Take him out! Sidorenko! Help him!

Krasnobruhov (resists them).—I won't go! I won't go if you drag me! Shave my head!

The Official.—Youshchenko! Give a hand! You'll go, all right.

Krasnobruhov (struggling).—Shave me! I'll complain. You have no right!

The Official.—Gavrilenko, carry him out!

Gavrilenko.—Get him by the leg! Catch him under the arms!

Krasnobruhov (struggling).—You won't carry me out!

The Official.—Go on, now!

(*The merchant is carried out with care and respect. The official smooths out his moustache and raises up his glass of tea, which proves to be cold.*)

The Official).—Vasilenko! A glass of hot tea! Oh, the deuce . . . Hot tea! Yes . . . Is the wounded man here?

Vasilenko.—He's dead now, your honor, dead and cold.

The Official.—Get out of here!

CURTAIN

[4]On the back of each convict's coat there is a badge, that resembles the ace of diamonds.—Translator's Note.

ANARCHY IN THE THEATRE

By Alfred Capus

Translated from the French by Barrett H. Clark

D URING the past fifteen years our dramatic literature has lost its appearance of regularity, so that to-day it is scarcely recognizable. We can discover no general end toward which it is striving, no school, no dominating influence. As a result, methodical souls are profoundly perturbed. There are people who insist that a play, a book, a picture, must immediately fall into some distinct category: the picture must belong to some school of painting, the book or the play to some definite literary genre. A work of art which does not so fit into their scheme of things appears to them an inferior creation. They are possessed by the mania for exact valuation and definite judgment. These people will never know the sweet joy, the poetry, of uncertainty. They are naturally very severe on the question of the contemporary stage, and it is they who have circulated the report that the drama is in a decline. Certain of them, less prompt to lose hope, are satisfied with saying that it is in a period of transition.

Since it is universally acknowledged that Corneille, Molière, and Racine will never again be equalled, and since every Frenchman is educated with this exasperating idea, it is evident that the decadence of the theatre began with the death of Racine, who was the last of the three in point of time. In proportion as we get away from these great masters does this decadence become apparent, and periods of transition succeed one another with regrettable haste. We must either take our stand in this matter, or else make up our minds not to repeat expressions which have been so abused that they have lost their original force.

What is and will always remain true, is that no classification of contemporaneous works is possible: there will always be a confusion of *genres* and an apparent disorder. Among the many principles which have recently suffered is that of the separation of *genres*. It was, however, a harmless principle and very convenient; it was a sure and ever-ready guide, enabling us to distinguish tragedy, tragi-comedy, comedy of character, comedy of manners, topical comedy, light comedy and vaudeville. Somewhere in the intervals between these *genres*, place was made, as a sort of refuge, for the thesis play and the family drama. Hard and fast rules for the drama were on the point of being formulated: order reigned in the halls of dramatic art. But suddenly anarchy made its appearance and, when it was least expected, the various forms were thrown into indescribable confusion. Comedies of manners appeared bordering on tragedy, and thesis plays that seemed at times like farces. These startling mixtures seemed made to disconcert; they gave place to new classifications: the social drama, the play of ideas, which served only to obscure the situation. If, for instance, a social drama is a play which portrays only the struggle between capital and labor, then there is not a play on marriage, the family, divorce, finance, which is not also a social drama. The term therefore is of no possible use in this new matter of classification.

Is it necessary to remark that the term " a play of ideas" is still more vague? Whenever a writer has some idea which he believes to be original on the subject of philosophy, politics, art, history, or science, he must impose on that idea the burden of lies and conventions of the stage, bend and torture it until it fits the rigid frame of the theatre, with all its tinsel, its trickery, and its false light; and he must of necessity lose his respect for his original idea. When the idea is not new, when the dramatist wishes to make it known to the public at large, his task is, I shall not say any less noble, but more personal, more intimate, as he is the go-between of the philosopher or the moralist. His business is to do what the philosopher cannot do, what the philosopher does not pretend to do: show men life with the aid of living beings; stir in them every sentiment, every passion, by means of the dramas of life which these sentiments and passions call forth; stir them in masses and force them to look at life for a little while in a sympathetic mood.

This does not mean that the dramatist should remain indifferent to the great realities of everyday life; if he wilfully ignores these, he will lose the greater part of his influence over the public of to-day. The various ideas and intellectual developments of the day, the ebb and flow of our ethical ideals, he must know and take into account. He must study with care the efforts which his generation is making to penetrate into the mysteries of knowledge, even though they be apparently foreign to his own art.   But the ideas which are floating about him should rather impregnate his work than become the principal end of it. They should likewise float about his characters, augment the intensity of their "scenic" life, and make them more "shaded," more real.

The oldest definition of a play is that it is an "animated representation of life."   That definition will never lose its significance.   But this representation, in order to be exact and in order to exercise the influence it should over a modern audience, has of recent years faced problems of all sorts, problems which dramatic art has not up to the present been forced to face.   Hence this appearance of hesitation and anarchy; for the first evidence of an irruption of this kind in the life of our time is to be observed in the contemporary stage; hence the incoherence and disorder. As I have said, the first of the time-honored principles to fall has been the principle of the separation of *genres*; nowadays *genres* are mixed, and so they shall remain, or if they are again separated into distinct groupings, the groupings will be far different from those of the past.   This principle was like a rigid frame which kept the writer well within certain defined limits.   It possessed the advantage of making unity and harmony easy to attain.   It indicated to the audience at once the precise direction in which the play was going and what way it was to end.   The spectator came to the theatre knowing what sort of play he was going to see; to-day that spectator is no more.   He was a being more distinct and recognizable than any we have to-day: he was either an aristocrat, merchant or tradesman, artisan, or workman. He felt himself separated from his neighbor by differences of education, class, and customs and manners.   In the theatre he occupied a place corresponding not only with his fortune, but above all, with his social status.   I shall not, however, pretend to assert that there are no longer any class distinctions or barriers between the classes.   The family that sits in the top gallery on a Sunday, and the group of fashionably-attired ladies, and gentlemen in dress-suits, who sit in one of the downstairs boxes, are undoubtedly separated in actual life by something far subtler and more complicated than a mere difference of fortune, but that difference is not the irreducible social difference.   In the course of a single generation, chance, education, and the continual metamorphoses of modern life can leap the gap, and that family in the top gallery in the next generation might well sit, not in the least surprised, as refined spectators in that main-floor box.

The mind of the theatre audience has profoundly changed during the past twenty years. What unexpected thrills run through it! What new contacts are felt! What subtle inter-communication between the different sections of that audience! What new types, what new states of mind, what mystery, are there! And how impossible it is to move them all with the same old tricks and the same old speeches!

Is it to be wondered at, therefore, that the drama, which is so impressionable, has radically changed its aspect? There is nothing more natural than that this public, the elements of which are constantly undergoing such marked changes, which has forgotten or nearly forgotten its class prejudices—which feels at least that it is on the point of forgetting them—which lives haphazard amid the tumult of changing ideas as naturally as it used to live in order and regularity—there is nothing more natural than that the public should not demand of dramatic art the same order, the adherence to outworn formulas, the facile division into *genres* and fixed forms. As it has forgotten its class prejudices, for the most part, so has it forgotten its prejudices against fixed forms. It judges now according to the personal and immediate emotional effect. It is willing to see on the stage any form that the dramatist chooses to employ: comedy or tragedy—or both at once. It is no longer superstitious on this point. Every possible conception of life, every point of view, is accepted beforehand, for the audience is aware that life to-day may present many aspects of itself at the same time. It cares little for schools and methods, provided the dramatist furnishes it with the sensations that are necessary, or those which surprise and interest, in a real and living play.

Provided you fulfil this requirement, you may mix your *genres*, violate every law, —no matter how many beautiful master-pieces have been written according to these laws. It must be borne in mind that the rules did not owe their origin to esthetic considerations alone: the theatre is bound by greater rules, by the very social laws which are so fatally intertwined with the stage. I might almost say that as the classes tend to intermingle more and more, and as individuals assume greater importance in life, so do the dramatic *genres* intermingle; and the drama tends to follow only such rules as are imposed upon it by the temperament and personal methods of the dramatist.

The theatres of Paris have undergone the necessary changes in quick order. Just consider for a moment, and you will see indications everywhere of this anarchy of which I speak. Where is the "Gymnase" style of play? Where is that of the "Palais-Royal?" Where are the special styles that were once seen on every boulevard? The Odéon has lost its distinction, and the Comédie Française, in its turn, has received and is now nobly bearing up under, the violent shock of the new generation.

This general anarchy of the theatre, which is an indubitable fact, cannot, without injustice, be considered a sign of decadence. It is the result of the prodigious efforts which have been made in every department of the theatre; efforts which will soon, I doubt not, evolve a new method of construction, a new way of developing; they will also reform the art of the actor and every branch of the mechanics of the stage.

New laws, new formulas, new *genres*, will probably take the place of the old ones; we shall soon be clear of this "transitional period," and once again order will reign for a time in the realm of the theatre.

SUNDAY ON SUNDAY GOES BY

By Henri Lavedan

Translated from the French by Mary Sibyl Holbrook

The FATHER, *a man of seventy-two, very erect, wearing the decoration of the Legion of Honor.*
The SON, *just twenty-four.*

In the month of August, on a bright sunny day. Both the above dressed as tourists, are standing on a little plateau out in the country: on either side, rather steep slopes, somewhat wooded, run down to a narrow river.
Father.—You know, my boy, I promised you that at the beginning of your twenty-fifth year, I would take you on a great journey.
Son.—It's my first one.
Father.—I am keeping my promise. We are in Alsace. We've done at a stretch, without stopping except to sleep a bit, the distance from Paris to Strasbourg, from Strasbourg to Nieder-bronn, by way of the Haguenau crossroads. Here we are at the gates of a village called Froeschviller. Look.
Son.—Yes.
Father.—And don't miss a single one of my words.
Son.—I am listening.
Father.—You know that place we came through an hour ago without getting out? The one you asked me the name of? It was Reichschoffen.
Son.—Reichschoffen.
Father.—That town over there in the plain is Woerth: the line of silver is the river Soultzbachel, flowing into the Sauer.
Son.—Oh! So it was here!
Father.—It was here, boy, in this place, twenty-seven years ago, on a Sunday morning, the seventh of August, that, after very nearly dying, I was taken prisoner.
Son.—You are going to show me the spot?
Father.—Yes. You were not born then, for I did not get

185

married until after I was out of prison and back in France. I had you very late. I wanted a son. For the revenge-to-be. When you were born I prayed God to let me live long to bring you when you had grown up to manhood, to the places where I had suffered the most. . . . . He has spared me. I thank him for it.

Son.—So do I, father.

Father.—I have told you the story of the battle. I won't go over all that again. Under what goes by the name of Reichschoffen there are three phases, Woerth, Froeschviller and Reichschoffen.

Son.—I know Woerth was the battle——

Father.—And a desperate one—desperate——

Son.—Froeschviller was the defeat——

Father.—It was, but a heroic one; defeat contested every inch of the way—our troops turned back on both wings, forced to give up one stand after another. And then from Froeschviller to Reichshoffen—

Son.—That was the rout.

Father.—Don't call it that. Say the retreat. And it was frightful, I can tell you. No more ranks kept—all arms confused and lost in the disorder and panic . . . . the dying falling on the dead, the artillery passing over the dying at a gallop—ghastly!

Son.—And what about the cuirassiers?

Father.—The cuirassiers?

Son.—Yes. Just what did they do in the fight?

Father—The cuirassiers represent two struggles, understand? Two supreme efforts risked, lost in advance, useless, sublime, two efforts that only Frenchmen make, one at Morsbronn. . . . .

Son.—And the other?

Father.—At Elsashausen. But we'll come to all that later . . . don't be impatient. I am going to take you over the ground of the manoeuvres. Our trip is young yet. It has only begun.

Son.—I wish it were done.

Father.—Why so?

Son.—Because it makes me feel sick already.

Father.—You are too sensitive, lad. You were talking of cuirassiers . . . you need to put some buckram in yourself. You aren't through yet.

Son.—Go on.

Father.—I was in command. My regiment was a part of the Third division, which was fighting the fifth Prussian Corps. The sixth of August fell on a Saturday—that spire you see is the Froeschviller church . . . but not the same one . . . it has been rebuilt. I'm telling you all this higgledy-piggledy, the memories fairly choke me. Look at that knoll over there—see it?

Son.—With a cross on it?

Father.—Yes. Oh! how it takes me back. It was there I stationed my main guard, the night before the battle. Nearly all night it rained steadily.(*He looks through his glasses*) And over there—what's that? More crosses? Your eyes are good.

Son.—Two, yes, three crosses. And still farther off, others still. What a lot there are.

Father.—Oh! You all but walk on them, here. They are a proverb, the crosses in this region. Not to mention the pyramids and the memorial statues. How many of my comrades are there! Poor old chaps. Friends I made at St. Cyr, where we trained— Anglade, who was Captain of the Turcos: De Bonneville—What's-his-name-that jolly dog that played the piano like a woman— I can't think of his name. Isn't that ridiculous? It will come to me. Yes, a lot of nice boys met a brave death here.

Son.—But what about you? That time you were in danger. You have never told me about it.

Father.—Purposely. I was keeping it to tell you when you were grown up, a man capable of understanding. Besides, it is nothing very serious. I'll tell the story now in a couple of words. Wounded by a bullet in the forehead, I lost consciousness and was left for dead on the battlefield, and not till next day did I come to my senses—the morning of the seventh. Stretched out in a furrow at the edge of the road, I was dreaming dimly of victory—of some glorious encounter or other—when a violent commotion shook me out of the torpor in which I had been sunken for the last sixteen hours. All at once I remembered. I opened my eyes. The sky was clear. I felt the earth damp with dew . . . . when suddenly I heard shooting. It was going on around me, almost on me. I expected to get my death-blow on the head close to the muzzle. I raised myself up and saw a Prussian kneeling and firing, with his gun resting on my chest, and as far as I could see, there were others—hundreds of them. Had the battle started up again? For a moment that was what I thought. But no. I may as well tell you right off, because you would never guess. Oh! what a nation! They were out

for practice. Do you get me? Training, if you please! Yes, on
the day after the victory, after hardly any rest at all they were
out manoeuvring on the field, on the real thing, still warm and
smoking, among the wounded, the dead, the debris, the severed
limbs. In the charnel-house, in the pools of blood mantled by
the chill of the night . . . those gentlemen were wading
about training their marksmen with blank cartridges, just for
nothing—merely not to get rusty. . . .

Son.—How disgraceful!

Father.—But what a lesson.

Son.—And then what happened?

Father.—I thought it was fighting. I stood up clutching a
cavalry-sword that I had found lying beside me, and had picked
up. The Prussians surrounded me, and I was bracing myself to
sell my skin for more than its worth, for all the world as if it had
been the skin of a major. I intended to stand my ground. The
fusillade had stopped. There were eight or ten of them upon
me—when, all at once—the clatter of a galloping horse. Up
rides a superior officer, who cries, "Hold on, there." They draw
aside. He salutes me: "Your sword, Captain. Allow *me* to
ask you for it." It was the Crown Prince. He was really very
decent.

Son.—And then?

Father.—I gave it to him, to be sure. I did not want to die.

Son.—Why not?

Father.—Because I wanted to have a son. Well, that's the
story. Stow it away in your knapsack. You know that after-
wards, when I was a prisoner . . . there were some rough
times too. (*At this moment the noise of drums is heard: the speaker's
features contract.*) But God forgive me—listen! One would
almost say . . .

Son (who is also listening intently).—Drums?

Father.—Yes . . . and the fifes. Those cursed fifes!

Son.—It must be they!

(*A peasant goes by.*)

Father (accosting the man).—Do you speak French?

*Peasant (coming up and guessing that he is speaking to a
soldier).*—Yes Captain.

Father (to his son, referring to the peasant).—Here's one now—
a genuine one. (*To the peasant, looking searchingly at him.*) So
it's still going on, is it?

Peasant.—All the time, Captain.

Father.—You're the right sort, my man. That's what we hear, I suppose?

Peasant.—Yes. Just now they are having manoeuvres.

Son.—They are coming nearer.

Peasant.—Here they are.

(*They come into sight at the end of the road. Their pointed helmets—the little flat drums—their booted thighs—now their brutal faces—can be seen—bull-dog jaws, green eyes with red lashes. And the sound of the fifes—sharp as knives that tear at the heart-strings.*)

Son.—Come on, father. Let us go.

Father.—No, stay? To-day, we can let them pass, but Sunday on Sunday is going by——

Son.—But with a difference.

Peasant.—Good-day to you.

Father.—Till we meet again.

(*The column marches away.*)

GIOVANNI PASCOLI

By Anne Simon

"The roses live by eating of their own beauty, and then die
. . . .
His song is the funeral chant for his own death of every moment."

AS I was reading for the first time Gabriele D'Annunzio's exquisite tribute to his brother-poet Pascoli, this couplet from Noguchi's poem, "The Poet," flashed through my mind with persistent recurrence. After longer meditation, I knew why the analogous association revealed itself to me. The Japanese poet and the Italian poet are intimately related by their love of Nature, and by their ability to see life always through eyes of wonder and surprise. Both of them seem reverent and almost breathless before the miracle of a blade of grass, the upward flight of the lark, the cry of the wind, and the exquisite beauty of each moment. It might not be quite clear to the casual reader, but nevertheless it is true that Pascoli's poetry was woven with the threads of sorrow; and it is equally true that his "funeral chant" reverberates through the structure of many of his poems. One realises that he felt this world was not his home; he seemed to suffer from a world-strangeness. Constantly searching for the inner reality, the soul of things, and being conscious of his inability to lay bare the reality behind the exterior, the inner soul, he was consumed by the "eating of his own beauty," and died. He was happy in touching visible things, yet always seemed to be looking for a casement out of which his soul might fly.

Quite accidentally I came across D'Annunzio's "Contemplation of Death." The book is divided into four sections, the first one being reminiscent of Pascoli. D'Annunzio, the exotic poet, pays to Pascoli, the gentle poet, a kind of homage that is both acute and affectionate. D'Annunzio's contemplation on Pascoli's death is written with a limpidity and charm that is most unusual. Something far more subtle and impressive emanates from this appreciation than has ever been evoked by any other biographical analysis of him. It is interesting to see that although it is D'Annunzian in treatment, yet it is surrounded by a distinctly Pascolian nebula. He writes with great nobility of word and phrase, and shows a deep sentiment in his friendship of which many considered him incapable. The entire essay is not only a beautiful thought, but is equally beautiful in its literary workmanship, and in the original, offers the reader many flawless pages. He has accomplished that most difficult and elusive thing; he has described a "state of soul," and surpassed even himself in the acquirement of a certain sort of admirable restraint.

Undoubtedly Giovanni Pascoli was one of Italy's greatest poets. He was born in 1855, at San Mauro, near Rimini, and on the last day of the year. If it is true that temperament is influenced or determined by the month of one's entrance into the world, then we can easily understand his pre-disposition to a gentle sort of melancholy and his intimate understanding of the anguish of the world.

He studied at Bologna under Carducci, and later had the honor of being his successor in the chair of Literature in the University of Bologna. He taught Greek and Latin, yet always with uneasiness and discomfort, for it seemed almost a profanation to be compelled to analyse the sacred pages of Virgil and Homer to mere children who looked upon them only as bridges necessary to education. D'Annunzio has called him "*Il Virgilio di nostro tempo*," and also "*L'ultimo figilio di Virgilio.*"

The following beautiful poetic tribute was written on the eve of D'Annunzio's exile from Italy, and evidently after Pascoli's death.

TO GIOVANNI PASCOLI

By Gabriele D'Annunzio

(*From "Alcioni," Libro III delle Laudi*)

My song, before I depart for my exile,
go along the Serchio, and ascend the hill
to the last son of Virgil, divine
offspring,

the one who understands the language of
the birds, the cry of the falcons, the
plaint of the doves, the one who sings
with a pure heart to the flowers as well as
to the tomb,

the one who dared to look earnestly
in the black and azure eye of the eagle
of Pella, and who heard the song of Sappho the beautiful
on the monsoon wind.

The son of Virgil rests silently
under a cypress and waits not for
thee. Fly! Thou art not brought by
the woman of Eresso, but thou cans't go alone;

he will receive thee with his generous
hand; he who perhaps was intent
on the alternation of his woof, or on
the bees, or "the late hour of Barga,"
or on his eternal verse.

Perhaps he has the book of his
divine parent on his knee (does he gather
now the lucky four-leaved clover

and use it to mark in his
book where Titiro sings, or where
Enea hears the response of Cumea
in the maze of the mountains?)

His sister with the smooth
hair has dropped her needles now
that it is late, and put away the linen
in the chest which is fragrant with
lavender.

Perhaps she is with him, sad because she
saw an ominous group of swallows on the
eaves. And thou O song, wilt say to him, "Son
of Virgil, here is the palm.

As an immaculate guest, thy dear brother, who is
about to depart, sends me to thee; for thy
noble head he shaped a garland with
his art."

And who today should crown the poet,
if not I myself, the poet of solitude?
The ignorant Scita and the masked
Medo are the sycophants of Glory;

and, if barbarity generates new monsters
on the wind, no more shall Febo Apollo
descend against this horror as castigator,
with his silver bow,

because thou, Poet, art the custodian
of the purest forms. With unflagging
pulse thy ancestral gentle blood
lives in all thy images.

Thy thought nourishes and illumines
men, just as the placid olive-tree
produces for man its pallid berry
that is both food and light.

Therefore accept this fraternal garland
that I, as messenger, bring thee.
It is not heavy . . . it is made of the
eternal frond, but it is very light.

It is made of a slender branch
that grew between the Alps and
the sea where that Heart of Hearts
found its savage pyre, and where
Buonarotti found his inspiration.

In the bending of the stem the
Artificer saw the ancient wounds
shine upon the Sagro and upon the
Altissimo the desired peplus of Nike.

Another invisible Mountain
ascend and that thou also ascendest but on the
opposite cliff. Alone, and far-away, an
immortal anxiety impels us both.

And did not our brave hearts
promise to meet one day,
on the summit? That
day, we will sing the same song
from the summit.

So, my song, tell him this. And
to his sister, whom thou mayst see
crying softly, give the last lily
of the sea that I gathered.

Pascoli was undoubtedly a great Latinist, and Virgilian in
spirit as well as in his scholasticism. He was the acknowledged
leader of the Classicists, but through no claim of his own. Al-
though he was permeated by classical tradition, yet he held the
people by his choice of subject as well as by his technique. He
was thirty-seven years old when he published his first volume of
poems.

In personality, he was modest and gentle; mentally he was
healthy and robust, and for this reason found himself secure in
his literary position, for at that time people were weary of trying
to penetrate the so-called obscurities of Carducci, and just as
impatient with the eroticism of D'Annunzio. He loved truth
and sincerity, passionately. D'Annunzio gives us a vivid
picture of his shyness, his reserved speech, and the simplicity of his
tastes. His most dominant trait was his love of Nature. His

love for birds is easily seen by scanning the titles of his poems
in the index. We may change slightly one of Hawthorne's
utterances and say, "his feeling for flowers and birds was very
exquisite, and seemed not so much a taste as an emotion."

Pascoli is not the poet for those who crave the delineation
of erotic things, but appeals strongly to those who care for sim-
plicity. He is thoroughly wholesome. He writes about humble
things, but he had that mystical power the real poet must have
—the power to invest these commonplace things with an aura
hitherto unseen by us.

THE NEST

From the wild-rose bush hangs the
skeleton of a nest. In the Spring what
joy used to come from it, making the
shore resound with the rapture
of the birds!

Now there is left only a feather, that
hesitates at the invitation of the wind. It
palpitates lightly, like an ancient dream
in an austere soul, always vanishing and
not yet vanished.

THE WHITE POPLARS

I see you again, O silver poplars,
bare in this autumnal day;
the morning mist foams lazily,
adorning each bud and branch.

The same wind that once opened the
buds, now whirls the yellow
leaves around. And I, at that time, cried,
"Go!" Now, my heart is full of tears.

Now the inert snows are on the mountains.
Now are the days of squalid rains.
Now the long anger, of the north wind pushes
against the door in the night.

Now are the brief days that seem
like infinite sunsets. Now are the days of
fading and fallen blossoms, and chrysanthemums,
the flowers of death!

THE SEA

I open my window and gaze
on the sea. The stars move
and the waves tremble. I see the stars fade away
and waves disappear. A gleam calls,
a throb answers. The water sighs, the wind breathes.
A beautiful silver bridge
suddenly appears over the sea. Bridge
arched over serene lakes, who made
thee, and whither dost thou lead?

After reading "Myricae," one feels that a new vision has
been created for the perception of the beauties of nature. In
one of his poems he said:

"I would like to spend my life clinging to the stem,
and reposing like dew on each petal."

He was truly a man of sorrow. In one year he suffered the
concentrated sorrow of a life-time. Nothing bitter ever permeat-
ed his poetry. He was the poet of the soul that suffers, but the
soul that has freed itself through suffering. One feels that he
was able by the alchemy of his art to fuse his sorrow and his
experience into his poetry.

ALL SOULS' DAY

How gloomy and sad is this day! In my
heart, I see a cemetery with a dark cypress tree
high above the walls.

And the haughty cypress now bends
before the sirocco; from time to
time the mass of clouds dissolves itself
in tears of rain.

O home of my people, my sad and only
home, O home of my fathers, my silent
home disturbed by tempest and flood;

O cemetery, cold and rough winters dost thou
give to my pale delicate mother, but
today I see immortelles

and chrysanthemums everywhere.
On each rust-stained cross hangs, as
if embracing it, a garland, from which
tears of rain are gently dropping.

. . . .

REMEMBRANCES

I

RIO SALTO

I know the sound that I heard
in the deep valley was not that made by
moving palfreys: it was only the water that
poured from the dripping tiles and
resounded in the gutter of the eaves.

And yet on the endless strand
I could see the knight-errants pass.
I discerned shining cuirasses,
and the shadow galloping upon the waves.

After the wind ceased, I no longer
heard the sound of galloping palfreys,
and I no longer saw flickering
distant flights in the uncertain light;

but you only I saw, my friendly poplar trees!
You rustled gently, waving
along the bank of my beloved river.

II

(To Severino Ferrari)

ROMAGNA

In my heart, Severino, there is always a
village and a field that smiles or weeps:
and the azure vision of San Marino
is always with me.

My heart constantly returns to that country
where reigned Guido and Malatesta,
and also the courteous Passator, king
of the street, king of the forest!

My heart always returns to the stubble
where the turkey-hen wanders with
another brood, where the rainbow-
colored duck paddles in the shining pool.

Oh! if I might be there!
And if I could lose myself
again in the verdure, 'midst elm-trees
full of nests and the birds, calling to each
other the cry that is lost in the
languor of noon,

when the peasant removes the scythe
from his shoulder and goes home to his
bowl of porridge, and the ox
in the dark stable enjoys his coarse
food.

From the scattered villages the bells
meanwhile answers each other with
silvery cries: they call to
shady places, to repose, to blessed
tables flowered with infantile eyes.

In those burning hours the lace umbrella
of the mimosa-tree, that flowered

my house in summer days with its plumes of
rose color sheltered me:

and thick bushes of rose and jasmine
were intertwined on the sheltered wall;
a tall and slender poplar watched
over everything, sometimes as noisy
as a street gamin.

It was my home: there I galloped often
with Guido Selvaggio and with Astolfo,
and when I imagined I saw before me the Emperor
in the hermitage.

And while I rode the
hippogriff in my dream, the words
of Napoleon resounded in my quiet room.

At the same time I heard amidst the fresh cut
hay the perpetual chirping of the crickets;
I heard from the frogs
in the ponds a long interminable
poem.

And long and interminable were those
poems that I meditated, beautiful to dream:
the rustling of leaves,
the song of birds, the smile of women,
the tumult of the sea.

But from that nest, like tardy
swallows, all of us migrated
one black day; for me, my country
is where I live; the others are
not very far away: in the cemetery.

And so I shall always
see on sultry days,
amidst the dusty hawthorne
the little ones of the lazy cuckoo.

sunny Romagna, sweet country,
where Guido and Malatesta reigned;
where the courteous Passator was
king of the street, king of the forest.

But he sings about Homerical things, also. His voice was
always gentle, and although he often touched depths, it was
only the depths of the lake—the silent lake, crossed by shadows.
It is true he used a very slender form, and he painted little things,
but his workmanship was very fine, and it was because of his
patient training in the really big issues of life—the training of
sorrow, endurance, and discipline.

He preached the independence of the soul, being himself
unwilling to be confined in a cage of any definite creed or philos-
ophy. In his "Ode to King Humbert" (who was killed while
reviewing the athletic societies, in the environs of Milan), he
wrote in the preface, "I dedicate this hymn to the young men
without party. I want to beg them to remain free . . life
is not dearer than freedom. I want them to fight for the eight-
hour law . . . to abominate political murders . . . to
raise the same hymn to the mason who falls from the scaffolding,
as to the soldier who dies embracing his cannon . . . Be
worthy of Dante, O ye sons of Dante!" He loved young Italy,
and implicitly believed in it.

FROM "THE FUNERAL HYMN OF KING HUMBERT"

Thou hast died standing, 'midst the sounds of the
hymn, for whose good one dies: with
good thoughts in thy heart, thou wert
struck in the heart:

thou hast passed away 'midst vivas shriller
than trumpets. In the wind amongst the
other banners, was the banner of Trent.

In that last evening on the field amidst
joyous enthusiasm, thou, O dead King,
didst review the young athletes.

Thou hast died on the field with thy hand
raised to thy austere forehead, seeing,
near and far, in that last evening,

in that last moment, with eyes
suddenly dimmed, a light shining
on the lances of the Uhlans with
eyes veiled by the shadow of Busca,

seeing a star shine midst the
menace of the storm; seeing New Italy
before thee.

With eyes so proud and sad thou
didst not see before this youthful
legion of athletes, the nocturnal Chimera
thirsty for blood,

that came hissing and panting and turning
towards the dead. Thou, King, wast
saluting the Italy of the Free and
the Strong,

sun-loving Italy, that demands
its perils and its praise, the
pickaxe and the trumpet, the
schools of thought, and the sonorous factories,

the Italy that hopes and works united
towards its bright goal, the Italy that shapes
its fate on the anvils,

the Italy that already opens up its
path towards the great future, that presses
always forward, be it towards peace or
war, San Giorgio or San Marco!

Thou did'st not see him: thou sawest only
the youthful athletes. The cry, "Do
your duty," ran serenely in their midst.

Thou sawest the stagnant marshes,
conquered by squalid heroes who
were brought back like war heroes
of old, only not on shields, but on hay.

And far away in a distant sea,
under harsh constellations, thou sawest
three ships fighting with perilous monsoons

Go! . . . steer for the Ideal!
Go! to the Ideal, whether it be a point
or a nothing; even if death bars the
way to it: but when thou arrivest . . . thou
art there.

Go, youthful prince of young Italy!
Into the labyrinth go, but seek thy
Pole; go find thy goal in the
infinite world!

Go, in the midst of the gray hurricane,
which seems like evening
but is suddenly transformed into a golden aurora.

August, 1900.

Pascoli wrote around very few root-ideas. He never lost
the divinity of the visible in striving to penetrate the poet's true
kingdom of vision. He craved quiet and solitude for his daily
work. An artist must seclude himself for a time in the caves and
deserts of the world of spirit or fantasy, and there, in his isolation,
is happy, and becomes finely creative. He had like Mallarmé,
a gift for the use of the most fitting word. He wrote with ex-
quisite lucidity and freshness of impression. He was somewhat
austere in his design and structure, and spoke in his poetry with
"the cloistral voice." He infuses into all his work a silvery
repose that is truly Virgilian. Was it Keats who said

"They shall be accounted poet-kings
Who simply tell the most heart-easing things."

If it is true that every work of art is a mirror in which we may see the image of its creator, then it is quite easy for us to see the real Pascoli in his poetry.

He was master of his art.   He was equally master of himself. He found his own centre, and dwelt there, and looked out on the world from an inner window, seemingly undisturbed by passing occurrences.   A disillusion to him was only a fresh spiritual impetus.

I always have the feeling in reading his poetry that he had constantly before him a thought that Victor Hugo once expressed: "We are all condemned, under sentence of death, but with an indefinite sort of reprieve."   In his "reprieve" he strove for two things—to touch Nature as intimately as possible, and to construct fairy palaces of exquisite thought for his refuge from the *Weltschmerz.*

He died April 6, 1912.   He was one of those souls whom Dante describes as "being made perfect by the workings of beauty."   Many people believed in him, and he was "a central fire descending upon many altars."

AN HUNGARIAN POET

BY ALICE STONE BLACKWELL

WILL some of the European monarchies become republics after the war? The hope is often expressed in America that this will be the case. There is a general belief that wars of conquest and aggression will seldom be undertaken by a nation which is democratically governed.

In one of the countries now at war, the songs of a republican poet have long been the delight of the whole people.

One of the most romantic figures in history is Alexander Petöfi, the beloved national poet of Hungary. It has been well said that his short life was one long romance. He sang and fought, like the troubadours of old; and he died fighting for freedom, in the flower of his youth. He was the idol of a brave and chivalrous nation while he lived, and now, two generations after his death, his songs are still household words in every home in Hungary.

The same songs sing themselves in the dumb hearts of the Hungarian workmen in America, as they toil in the factories and mines, cut off from the comprehension of their fellows by a little-known tongue.

Petöfi was born in 1823, in the early hours of New Year's morning. His parents were poor, his father having lost most of his possessions in an overflow of the Danube. The father was a good, simple-hearted man, a butcher by trade. Petöfi's mother has been described as "one of nature's noble ladies." Her son said: "She was full of poetry. I drank it in the milk of her bosom. I learned it from her smiles and tears."

The boy was educated in the evangelical parochial schools. He began early to write verses, but did not distinguish himself as a student. From his childhood he had a passion for the drama. While at boarding school, he slipped off and went to see a band of strolling German players. This was a flagrant breach of the rules, and the head of the school wrote to Petöfi's father that his son was "a hopeless dunce and good-for-nothing."

After this disgrace, the boy ran away. He went to Buda Pest, hoping to enter the National Theatre, but could get employment only as an obscure "supe." For a time he tramped the country as a vagrant, and finally enlisted in the Austrian army. He thought the regiment was about to be ordered to Italy, and he longed to see the country of Horace. Instead, it was sent to the Tyrol. He saw years of hard service, during which he suffered from want, abuse, and the petty despotism of narrow-minded superiors. Still his head was full of poetry, and he scribbled verses all over the walls of his room, and constantly recited them. In 1841 the regimental physician, a great admirer of Petöfi's poems, delivered him from this life of slavery by declaring him invalided. He went home, and was received with joy by his parents; but he could not fall in with his father's wish to make him a butcher. He went to college for a time, and took a prize for a lyric poem; but still the theatre allured him. For years he roved the country, acting with strolling bands of players, and always having poor success. He almost starved. Meantime he was beginning to be known as a poet, and at length he got a position as editor of a literary journal. He made one final struggle for success as an actor, in the National Theatre, and failed decisively. From that time on, he gave himself to his true vocation, that of a poet. In rapid succession he sent out volume after volume of poems, which went straight to the hearts of the people. His songs were sung everywhere, in the palace and in the hovel; by college students and illiterate peasants; by the artisans in the workshops, and the farmer ploughing his field. It is said that Petöfi seldom woke in the morning or lay down at night without hearing the people singing his songs in the streets.

Petöfi was showered with honors. He was given the freedom of ancient cities. In the National Theatre, where he had suffered fiasco as an actor, he saw the whole audience rise on his entrance and cheer him till he had taken his seat. His arrival in any town was the signal for a fête or a torchlight procession. These demonstrations were trying to his modesty, and when he saw that a big crowd had turned out to receive him, he would often enter by back streets to avoid them.

Petöfi's character was as lovable as his genius was uncommon. Through all the vicissitudes of his roving and adventurous career, he kept a clean heart and an upright life. In his more than three thousand poems, there is not a word offensive to purity.

He was incorruptibly honest, brave and sincere. In his

mind, integrity of character was closely linked with his political principles, which he cherished with passion. He wrote in his diary on April 19, 1848:

"I am a republican, body and soul. I have been one ever since I learned to think, and I shall be one till my latest breath. These strong convictions, in which I have never wavered, pressed into my hand the beggar's staff that I carried for so many years. During the time when souls were bought and paid for in hard cash, when a devoutly-bent body secured a man's future, I shunned the market, and bowed to no one, but stood erect, and froze and suffered hunger. Never have I hired out even a string of my lute or a stroke of my pen. I sang and I wrote that to which the God of my soul prompted me; but the God of my soul is liberty."

Again in the diary he wrote: "The motto of a true republican is not 'Down with kings!' but 'Pure morality!' Not the crushed crown, but irreproachable character and upright honesty are the foundations of the republic. With these, you shall fell monarchies to the earth as David felled Goliath."

Petöfi fully believed, however, that crowns ought to be crushed. He has a very fiery poem, the burden of which is "Hang up the kings!"

"I am a republican out of religious conviction," he wrote. "The men of monarchies do not believe in the development, the advancement of the world, or else they want to check them; and this is infidelity."

In 1846 Petöfi married Julia Szendrey, a beautiful girl, of a rich and distinguished family. She accepted the butcher's son against her parents' will, and gave up wealth and ease to live with him in a plain little lodging adorned only with portraits of the leaders of the French revolution. These pictures, handsomely framed, were Petöfi's one luxury.

The marriage was ideally happy. The great Hungarian novelist, Maurus Jokai, an intimate friend of the poet, has given a sketch of their domestic life in "Eyes like the Sea," a story in which Petöfi appears as one of the characters:

"The furniture was very primitive. Mrs. Petöfi had left her father's house without a dowry; she had not so much as a fashionable hat to bless herself with; she had sewed herself together a sort of head-dress of her own invention. They had nothing, and yet they were very happy. Julia's sole amusement was to learn English from Petöfi. At dinner (which was sent in from 'The Eagle'), we spoke English, and laughed at each other's blunders."

Petöfi joined with heart and soul in the war for national independence. At the beginning of the revolution, in the spring of 1848, he wrote his "Talpra Magyar!" ("Up, Magyar, up!") which became the foremost war song of Hungary:

Up, Magyar, up, your country calls!
    This is the fateful day.
Shall we be freemen or be serfs?
    It is for you to say!

We take an oath of freedom,
    We swear it o'er and o'er;
We swear by the God of the Magyars
    We will be serfs no more!

Our sires were free in life and death,
    Their souls are not at ease;
They suffer; in a land of serfs
    They cannot rest in peace.

A vagrant with no fatherland
    Is he who now shows fear—
Who than his country's honor holds
    His worthless life more dear.

The sword is brighter than the chain,
    Yet chains till now we wore;
The good sword decorates the arm—
    Be ours our sword of yore!

The Magyar name shall shine again
    Worthy its ancient fame;
The long disgrace of centuries
    We'll wash from off that name.

Our grandsons, where our green graves rise,
    Some day shall prostrate fall,
And, breathing blessings in their prayers,
    Our sacred names recall.

> We take an oath of freedom,
>   We swear it o'er and o'er;
> We swear by the God of the Magyars
>   We will be serfs no more!

Petöfi was elected a member of the National Diet, but soon enlisted in the army. He became secretary and aid-de-camp to General Bem, who loved him enthusiastically, and asked to have Petöfi's poems read to him on his death-bed. Petöfi aided the revolution by drawing up calls and manifestos, as well as by writing war songs, which were read to the soldiers, and received with acclamations. He fell in the battle of Segesvar, July 31, 1849, at the early age of twenty-six.

Petöfi's poems have been tra slated into French, German, Italian, English, Polish, Danish and Flemish. One of his biographers says that there are good translations in every language but English. The fact that the English versions have not been considered very successful warrants another attempt to bring some of these poems within the reach of English-speaking readers. The music and grace of Petöfi's verse are necessarily lost in translation; but it is hoped that something of the beauty and originality of his thought may shine out, even through the imperfections of the English rendering.

Petöfi wrote many love-songs. The following are examples:

ACROSS THE WATER

> The river has o'erflowed its banks;
>   Beyond it stands thy cot.
> The countryside is flooded wide—
>   My rose, expect me not!
> The causeway and the bridge are gone,
>   They vanished like a dream;
> Now the last fragments of the bridge
>   Are floating down the stream.
>
> Upon a hill I stand and gaze
>   Far to the other side.
> A dove is flying on swift wings
>   Across the waters wide.

I know not if that flitting thing
   A real dove may be,
Or if perchance it is a sigh
   Breathed from my heart toward thee!

THE WHEAT IS RIPENING

The wheat is ripening in the field; hot, hot the bright days grow.
On Monday I shall start to reap, with morning's earliest glow.

My love is ripening too, because my heart is hot in me.
My dear, my one and only dear, do thou its reaper be!

FALLOW IS MY STEED

Oh, fallow is the color of my steed!
His hair is like the gold that glitters bright.
"Star" is the name of this good steed of mine;
His feet are swift as falling stars at night.
Heigho, my beauteous horse, my fallow steed!
One of your shoes, where is it gone?   Who knows?
Come, let me take you to the smith, my steed,
And then do you take me to see my rose.
Oh, fiery is the charcoal of the smith!
In my love's eyes a glow more ardent lies.
Soft is the iron before the charcoal's fire,
Softer my heart beneath my truelove's eyes.

A LOVERS' QUARREL

My rose, she gave me deep offence,
And oh, my wrath was sore!
Yes, I was angered, I was grieved,
As many a time before.
I thought the grave-digger alone
Could cure the hurt she gave;
I thought my wound would not be closed
Till opened was my grave.

My pain, how long did it endure?
Until her first sweet kiss.
Soon as my angel kissed my lips,
My grief was changed to bliss.
A pointed poniard is her word,
Her lip a balsam sweet.
So are these girlish creatures made;
Their power how can we meet?

CLOUD AND SUN

High, high the cloud is flying;
    Far, far is she, my rose.
The cloud flies westward, westward;
    Westward the warm sun goes.

Fly o'er her, cloud, and say I bear
    A mournful heart, like you!
Haste, burning sun, and say to her
    My heart is burning too!

HAPPY NIGHT

O happy night! I now am with my rose.
Together in the little garden-close
We find the time fleet swiftly. All is still
Save for dogs barking. In the sky o'erhead
The moon and stars their magic lustre shed,
As in a fairy tale, o'er vale and hill.

I never should have been a good star, I;
God knows, I could not have remained on high!
I should not ask in heaven's realm to be,
But when the twilight shadows gathered brown,
As soon as evening fell I should come down,
My rose, my rose belovèd, unto thee!

A LOVER'S HASTE

Come, let me saddle you, my trusty steed;
    This very day I must be with my love.
My left foot scarce is in the stirrup yet,
    But even now my heart is with my dove.

Yon bird is flying—to his mate, perchance;
    Fleetly he flies, and he outstrips our gait;
Let us o'ertake him swiftly, my good steed,
    Not even he can better love his mate.

I LOVE YOU

I love you, my sweetheart, with depth and with might!
I love your dear figure, so little and light;
I love your black tresses, your forehead of snow,
Your dark eyes, your cheek with its roseate glow;
That lip, sweet and red, so delightful to kiss;
That soft little hand, whose mere touch is my bliss;
The flight of your soul, soaring lofty and free,
The depth of your heart, like the deeps of the sea.
I love you when merry, and when you are sad,
Your teardrops as much as your smiles blithe and glad.
Your virtues' pure brightness I love, yet 'tis true,
The eclipse of your failings is dear to me too.
I love you, my sweetheart, all others above,
As much as a human heart ever can love.
No life and no world exist for me save you;
In the warp of my thoughts you are woven all through.
Of each feeling, awake or in dreams, you are part:
You speak in each pulse, in each throb of my heart.
All glory for you I would gladly resign;
All glory for you I would win and make mine.
No wish and no will remains to me to tell,
For whatever you will, that is my will as well.
The costliest sacrifice, e'en of my all,
If pleasure it gave you, would seem but too small;
And the veriest trifle to me were a cross,
And would fill me with pain, if you grieved for its loss.
I love you, my sweetheart, I love and adore

As never, no, never has man loved before.
I well nigh am slain by this love, great and true;
And I in one person am all, all to you,
Who ever can love you, and for you live on—
Your husband, your brother, sire, lover and son;
And you in one person are all to my life—
My daughter, my mother, love, sister and wife.
I love with my soul and I love with my heart,
With a love mad and wild, that shall never depart.
If there be any praise for this love deep and true,
It still is not I who deserve it, but you.
The praise and reward should be yours, O my dove,
For 'tis you that have taught me this great, mighty love!

Petöfi had a keen feeling for the beauties of nature:

IN AUTUMN

The autumn has returned once more to earth,
   As beautiful as ever to mine eyes.
God knows the reason why, but in my heart
   The autumn days I always love and prize.

Upon the hilltop now I sit me down,
   And let my glances wander far around,
And listen to the leaves that from the trees
   Are dropping with a faint and gentle sound.

Smiling, the Sun upon the Earth beneath
   With mild and tender beam looks down the while;
So on her infant, as it falls asleep,
   A loving mother gazes with a smile.

Falling asleep, not dying, is the Earth,
   In mellow autumn, with its silence deep;
And even by her eyes we may perceive
   She is not ill, but heavy with soft sleep.

She has but laid aside her rich attire,
   Unrobing slowly, without haste or pain;
She will re-clothe herself when breaks her day—
   When to the world the spring returns again.

Sleep on, O Nature, fair and beautiful!
    Until the morn, sleep on and take your rest,
And in your slumber dream upon the things
    That in your waking hours you love the best!

Just with a finger's tip I touch my lyre,
    Softly I play, scarce louder than a sigh.
My gentle, slow and melancholy song
    Sounds on the still air like your lullaby.

Sit down beside me, angel of my heart!
    Sit here by me in silence for my sake,
Until my song shall drift away and die
    As dies the whispering wind across a lake.

And when you kiss me, on this autumn day,
    Press your lips gently, slowly upon mine.
Oh, let us not, by sudden word or sound,
    Wake sleeping Nature from her dream divine!

There are many poems of sentiment:

THE FLOWERS OF THE VALLEY

The flowers of the valley, they still are in blossom,
The poplars outside of the window are green:
But look how the winter is touching the landscape!
White snow on the peaks of the mountain is seen.

Within my young heart there is fire-flaming summer,
And all the spring blooms there, in purple and red;
But, see, my dark hair is beginning to whiten;
The frost of the winter is touching my head.

The blossom is falling, and life too is passing.
Come sit here, my wife, on my knee, in your bloom!
Oh, you that to-day rest your head on my bosom,
To-morrow, perchance, will you kneel at my tomb?

Oh, tell me, if I should die first, will you cover
My face, while the tears from your eyelids shall break?

And will a youth's love, on some day in the future,
Persuade you to give up my name for his sake?

If ever you cast off the widow's veil, place it
That day on my grave, like a dark flag, I pray;
From the world of the tomb I shall come back to get it
At midnight, and with me shall bear it away,

To wipe my tears, flowing for you who thus lightly
Forgot your true liegeman, so faithful of yore,
And to bind up the wounds of this heart, which will love you
That day as it now does, and will evermore.

THE OX TEAM

What I shall tell you did not chance in Pest;
 Things so romantic do not happen there.
Once an aristocratic company
Within a cart were seated, free from care.
'Twas in an ox-cart that they jogged along;
 Four oxen made their team, and they were gay.
Along the high road, followed by the cart,
 The oxen, pacing slowly, took their way.

The night was bright. Above them shone the moon;
 Pale 'mid the wind-rent clouds she wandered slow,
Like a sad lady in a graveyard lone,
 Seeking her husband's grave with face of woe.
A merchant breeze called on the neighboring meads
 And bought sweet scents where'er its wings might stray.
Along the high road, followed by the cart,
 The oxen, pacing slowly, took their way.

Amid that company I too was there;
 Elizabeth was seated next to me.
The other members of our little band
 Were talking loud and singing merrily.
I mused; then to Elizabeth I said:
 "Shall not we choose a star? What dost thou say?"
Along the high road, followed by the cart,
 The oxen, pacing slowly, took their way.

"Shall we not choose a star to be our own?"
　Dreamily to Elizabeth I said.
"The star will lead us back to happy thoughts,
　To memories of days forever fled,
Should fortune part us in the years to come."
　And so we chose a star our own to be.
Along the high road, followed by the cart,
　Went the four oxen, pacing stolidly.

A PLAN THAT FAILED

Still, as I journeyed toward my home,
　I thought, "When I shall see
My mother's face, so long unseen,
　What shall my first words be?

"What beautiful and tender thing
　Shall first of all be said,
When she holds out to me the arms
　That rocked my cradle bed?"

And thoughts, each lovelier than the last,
　Come flocking manifold,
Till time with me seemed standing still,
　Though on my carriage rolled.

Into the little room I stepped;
　My mother flew to me—
And speechless from her lips I hung,
　Like fruit upon its tree.

THE BELLS HAVE CEASED

The evening bells have chimed and sunk to silence;
　Their notes died long ago.
Who is it that at this late hour still wanders,
　Mute, sad and slow?
Alone I wander through the silent village;
　I roam at will.

I wander, looking for my dream!   The vision
    Eludes me still.
The moon is up above me in the heavens,
    And in the skies
The stars are shining, shining, like so many
    Fair maidens' eyes.
Two storks upon the roof-tree of yon dwelling
    Have built their nest;
Two persons sit below them in the doorway,
    Together pressed.
A youth and maid, one fair, one dark, they sit there
    Absorbed, and take no note.
The lad around his little lass wraps gently
    His sheepskin coat.

I passed them by; they did not even mark me,
    Nor hear, nor see.
O Lord my God, how happy and how blissful
    Those two must be!
I grudge them not their bliss—yet notwithstanding,
    Would I were he
Who puts his arm around that small brown maiden
    So tenderly!

I WALK ABROAD

I walk abroad this autumn day,
But o'er the land is thrown
A veil of cloud; in vain I gaze—
The church-spire shows alone.

Nature is a forsaken church;
Its worshippers, the flowers,
Are gone, and hushed its organ tones—
The birds amid the bowers.

But Nature's silent church again
Shall ring with music high,
As 'twere an echo of the spring,
When autumn days draw nigh.

The vintage is a merry thing!
Oft would my heart repine:
"I too would pluck the ripened grapes;
Why is no vineyard mine?"

One cluster now would be enough;
For vineyards naught I care.
You would suffice me, little girl,
Cluster most sweet, most fair!

Petöfi has been called "the Burns of Hungary." Many
of his poems illustrate Hungarian life and character, like "A
Little Tavern:"

Where the village ends, a little tavern
Stands beside the Szamos, flowing clear.
It could see its image in the water,
Only that the night is drawing near.

Night is falling, with its dim gray shadows;
All the world is growing hushed and still.
By the shore the ferry boat is resting,
Darkness fills it, silent, mute and chill.

But the inn is noisy, and the player
Smites the cimbalon with might and main,
And the lads so lustily are shouting
That the windows quake in every pane.

"O my hostess, golden flower of women!
Bring me your best wine, that brightest flows.
Let it be as aged as my grandsire,
And as ardent as my youthful rose!

"Play up, gipsy,* play up louder, better!
I am in the mood to dance to-day.
Madly now I dance away my money,
Madly now I dance my soul away!"

*In Hungary the gipsies are the musicians of the people.

Somebody comes knocking at the window:
"Don't make such a noise! More quiet keep.
'Tis his lordship sends this message to you;
He has gone to bed and wants to sleep."

"Oh, I say, the devil take his lordship!
You may follow too, the selfsame way.
Never heed him, gipsy, keep on playing,
Even if I sell my shirt to pay!"

"Lads, God bless you!"—Somebody comes tapping
Once again before the hour takes flight—
"Please amuse yourselves a bit more softly;
My poor mother is not well to-night."

No one answers, but they drain their glasses,
And they bid the music cease to play;
And, as quickly as their wine is finished,
All the lads are on their homeward way.

GREEN LEAVES

Green leaves and snowy blossoms
On the acacia tree!
Below, a little fair-haired girl
All dressed in blue I see.
A shower of rain is falling,
She waits till it be o'er;
Meanwhile I cast sheep's eyes at her
From under our porch door.

Come in, my little pigeon!
Enter our room and rest.
Until the rain be over
Sit down upon our chest.*
On to the chest I'll lift thee up
If 'tis too high for thee;
Or, if the seat shall seem too hard,
I'll take thee on my knee.

*In Hungary a large chest is part of the furniture of every peasant house.

Petöfi's chivalrous spirit toward women is shown in "Cloud and Star:"

When God the Father had created man,
   His brow grew very dark, I know not why;
And from His forehead's darkness there were born
   The clouds and thunders of our earthly sky.
But when the woman God our Lord had made,
   Ah, then he wept with tears of pure delight!
Those tears of joy, you may behold them now,
   The myriad lovely stars that gem the night.

Love and war are dominant themes in Petöfi's poems. He placed as motto on the title page:

Freedom and love, these two I prize
All other things above.
For love, I sacrifice my life;
For liberty, my love.

Love and patriotism sometimes had a hard struggle in his breast:

WHY DO YOU FOLLOW ME?

Why do you follow me at every step,
O ever-busy love of fatherland?
Why do you show me always, day and night,
Your mournful face, and still before me stand?
You haunt me evermore, in sorrowing guise;
I see you even when I close my eyes.

Let me forget I am a citizen!
The spring has come, the world is blooming fair,
The flowers are fragrant, and the gladsome birds
Fill earth and heaven with song that thrills the air;
The golden clouds, benignant spirits, spread
Their bright shapes joyously above my head.

Let me forget I am a citizen!
Youth and a worshipped sweetheart I possess;
Hours set in pearls are offered to me now

By youth and love, a gift my heart to bless;
And every hour I do not take and kiss,
I waste a whole eternity of bliss.

Ah, Youth and Spring and Poesy and Love!
How many fairies all together stand!
And shall I let them fly away from me?
Yearning for them, to them I stretch my hand.

Come to me, reach to me your arms, I pray;
Embrace me, fairies, I am yours today!

Many of Petöfi's poems are exceedingly martial. While the revolution was brewing, he wrote:

I dream, I dream of bloody days
That whelm the world in ruin dread,
And on the old world's ruins drear
Create a bright new world instead.

Would they but shout, would they but shout,
The trumps of war, the voice of fate!
The battle sign, the battle sign
My eager heart can scarce await.

How merrily upon that day
Shall I into my saddle spring,
And 'mid the scores of warriors go
With wild joy swiftly galloping!

And if the foemen pierce my breast,
There will be one the wound to dress—
One who will close it with a kiss,
And heal it with a sweet caress.

If in a prison cell I lie,
Someone will come, past bolt and bar,
To make the prison's darkness bright
With eyes that match the morning star.

If I shall die, if I shall die
On scaffold or on battle plain,
There will be one who with her tears
Will wash my corpse from bloody stain.

The martial note in Petöfi's poems may jar upon those who
recognize in the call to "war against war" one of the supreme
appeals to twentieth-century chivalry. But it was characteristic
of the time, the country and the man. Petöfi speaks of freedom
as the only thing worth fighting for, and declares that all men have
been insane who ever gave their lives in battle for any other
cause. His creed on the question of war and peace is summed up
in these stanzas:

Peace, peace be unto all the world,
But ne'er by tyrants' will!
Only from Freedom's holy hands
Let peace the broad earth fill.

If universal peace on earth
In this wise there may be,
Then let us cast our arms away,
And sink them in the sea.

But, if not so, arms, arms till death,
A never-ending fray!
Yes, even if the war shall last
Until the Judgment day!

Petöfi longed to die for freedom:
The thought of war has ever been
The dream most dear to me—
War, where this heart might sacrifice
Its life for liberty.

This idea recurs again and again:

One thought alone brings sorrow to my heart—
To die upon my pillows, in my bed!
Slowly to fade away, as fades a flower
On which a worm in secrecy hath fed;

Slowly to perish, as a candle dies
  That stands within a lonely, empty room—
Give me not such a death, O Lord, my God!
  Let no such pathway lead me to the tomb!

Let me be like a tree by lightning struck,
  Or from the earth uprooted by the blast—
A rock that from the mountain to the vale
  By some terrific thunderbolt is cast!

When all the peoples that in slavery groan,
  Tired of their yoke, flock to the place of swords,
With flushing cheeks, and banners red unfurled,
  And bearing on those flags the sacred words:

"Freedom for all the world!"—when this is cried,
  And shouted far and wide, from East to West,
And tyranny encounters with their hosts,
  There may I fall, there may I sink to rest!

There let the young blood of my heart gush forth,
  And let the clash of swords, the ring of steel,
Drown the last shouts of joy that pass my lips,
  Lost in the trumpet's note, the cannon's peal!

And over my dead corpse let snorting steeds
  Gallop to victory, rushing like the wind,
And, crushed beneath the trampling of their hoofs,
  Let me upon the plain be left behind.

There let them gather up my scattered bones
  When the great burial day shall come at last,
When, to slow, mournful music's solemn notes,
  And with veiled banners waving in the blast,

The soldiers shall be carried to their rest,
  And to one common tomb consigned shall be
The heroes who have fallen in the fight,
  Oh, sacred Freedom of the World, for thee!

This poem seems prophetic. Petőfi's body was never found.
It was believed to have been trampled beyond recognition by the

charge that swept over him after he had fallen. He was buried with the unrecognized dead.

The following poem written not long before his death, has especial interest in this year of battles:

THE BATTLEFIELD

Oh, who would think or who would say
That this was once a battlefield—
That here, a few short weeks ago,
Blood flowed and war's loud thunder pealed?

'Twas here we fought; around us here
The foe his armèd legions spread;
'Twas death before and death behind,
An awful day, a day of dread!

Then, like the sorrow of a man,
Morose and gloomy was the sky;
Now it is mild and purely blue
As is an infant's limpid eye.

Then, like an old man's wintry head,
The earth was white with snow's chill sheen;
Now, like a youth's upspringing hope,
'Tis bright with hues of living green.

Then the deep clangor of a bell
Was booming in the atmosphere.
Now in the air above my head
The lark is singing blithe and clear.

Then here upon the field we saw
The blood-stained corpses of the slain;
But where the dead were lying thick
Now flowers are blooming on the plain.

Oh, who would think or who would say
That this was once a battlefield—
That here, a few short weeks ago,
Blood flowed, and war's wild thunder pealed?

Petöfi fully realized that courage is needed not in war alone. While Hungary was still at peace, he wrote "Ragged Heroes:"

I too could dress my verses up
    In rhymes and metres fair,
As fits when we go visiting
    In fashion's pomp and glare.

Songs —

But my ~~thoughts~~ are not idle youths
    Who for amusement live,
To go, in gloves and well-curled locks,
    Calls to receive and give.

No sword rings now, no cannon booms;
    Dim rust has quenched their rage;
Yet war goes on; instead of swords,
    Ideas the battle wage.

Among your warriors, O my Time!
    I combat as I can.
'Tis by my poems I contend;
    Each is a fighting man.

Ragged but valiant lads are they,
    All brave in battle's press.
A soldier's duty is performed
    By courage, not by dress.

Whether my poems will survive
    I do not ask at all;
If in this battle they perchance
    Must perish, let them fall.

This book that holds my dead ideas
    E'en then will sacred be,
Because of heroes 'tis the grave
    Who died for liberty!

But the poems have lived, and will live while the Hungarian people and Hungarian literature survive. Nor has their influence been confined to the poet's compatriots. They have helped to arouse the spirit of liberty in many lands. Béranger admired them; Heine declared that Petöfi's "rustic song is sweeter than the nightingale's." Every lover of freedom, of poetry and of chivalry feels the richer after making acquaintance with Petöfi. As eloquence is more telling when there is " a man behind the speech," so Petöfi's songs of freedom are the more inspiring because behind them stands that youthful and knightly figure, "without fear and without reproach." He shines like a star in the history of that dark and bloody time.

THE TOWN

By Theodor Storm

Translated from the German by P. H. Thomson

By the gray shore, by the gray sea,
    The old town lies alone;
On its roofs the fog weighs heavily,
And round the silent town the sea
    Sounds its dull monotone.

No woodland murmurs, no May-sprite
    Sings on with never an end;
Only the migrant geese in flight
Honk shrilly through the autumn night;
    The reeds bend in the wind.

Yet all my heart is on thy shore,
    Gray town beside the sea;
Light of my youth forevermore
Lies over thee and thy lone shore,
    Gray town beside the sea.

BLOOD

BY MARY CAROLYN DAVIES

God of death, Let my breath
To sword and spear belong!
(But ever the cry of the people saith, a song, a song!)
Lord of life, give me strife!
Make my right arm strong!
(But the cry of the people day and night, a song, a song!)
Strike the blow, hate the foe, never cease from smiting,
For blows the hands of a man are made, fighting, fighting;
And the shoulders high of a man are good as they press on through
    the throng
(But ever the lips of the people cry, a song, a song!)

God on high, See they fly!
God, thy ark is here!
(And ever the moan of the folk is blown, a song, a song!)
God! To you, praise anew,
For strength behind the spear!
(And the cry of the people gaunt with woe, a song, a song!)
Swing the sword, say no word, never cease from swinging,
Men we be, blood is free, where is use for singing?
For the lips of a man are sold to blood and his eyes to hate belong.
(But ever the hearts of the people cry, a song, a song!)

FAIR ROHTRAUT

By Eduard Mörike

Translated from the German by P. H. Thomson

King Ringang's daughter, what is her name?
    Rohtraut, Fair Rohtraut.
What is she doing all the day,
Who dare not spin as others may?
    She's fishing and hunting.
Oh, would I might her huntsman be!
Fishing and hunting were joy to me!
    —Hush, heart of mine, hush thee!

And it came to pass ere many a day,
    Rohtraut, Fair Rohtraut,
In Ringang's castle served the lad,
A huntsman's coat and a steed he had,
    To ride with Rohtraut.
If I were a king's son it might be,
Rohtraut, Fair Rohtraut would marry me.
    —Hush, heart of mine, hush thee!

Once they were resting beneath an oak,
    Then laughed Fair Rohtraut:
Why look you so fondly at me there?
Come hither, kiss me if you dare.
    Ah, the boy was frightened!
But he thought: I may, she will not resist.
The mouth of Fair Rohtraut he kissed.
    —Hush, heart of mine, hush thee!

Then home they rode, nor spake a word,
    Rohtraut, Fair Rohtraut;
But a song in his young heart sang of her:
Today, were you wed to the Emperor,
    It would not grieve me:
Ye thousand leaves on the branches wist—
The mouth of Fair Rohtraut I have kissed!
    —Hush, heart of mine, hush thee!

THE SEVENTH SOLITUDE

FROM NIETZSCHE'S DIONYSOS-DITHYRAMBS

Translated from the German by L. M. Kueffner

Great day of my life!
  the sun sinks.
The smooth sea lies
  all gilded now.
Warm breathes the cliff:
  slept there, at noon,
Life's joy its noonday sleep?
  In green lights, still,
Joy dances up the abyss.

Golden serenity come!
  You, O secret
O sweetest foretaste of death!
Have I wended my way too fast?
For not until now, when weary my foot,
  has your glance found me out,
  has your Joy found me out.

All around me but waves and their play.
  And whatever seemed heavy once,
Into blue forgetfulness now it has sunk—
  and idle stands my skiff.
Passage and storm—no longer it knows—
  Drowned are wishing and hoping,
  smooth lie soul and sea.

Seventh Solitude!
  Never before have I felt
sweet security nearer,
or warmer the sun.
Are not my peaks still a-glow?
  Silvery, light, a fish,
  sea-ward my skiff swims now. . .

THE POOL

By Annette von Droste-Hülshoff

Translated from the German by P. H. Thomson

How still it lies in the sunlight there,
Like a good conscience, self-complacent;
If zephyrs kiss it, banks adjacent
And the little flowers are unaware;
Dragon-flies hover over it,
Slender, blue-gold and carmine-lit;
Across its sheen the spiders go
In fitful mazes, to and fro;
The yellow iris lifts aloft
Her coronal, to catch the whisper,
The crooning in the grasses, soft:
Peace, seems the burden of each lisper.

Oh, hush, it sleeps, be quiet, quiet
Whir softly, golden dragon-fly,
Temper your pinions shrilling riot;
Reeds on the bank, keep watchful eye,
And let no pebble fall to waken.
On a fleecy cloud it has its bed,
And lullabies are lightly shaken
Out of the old tree overhead;
A little bird, on pinions slow,
Sails high above in sunlit spaces,
And like a darting fish, below,
Its shadow through the water races.

Hush, hush! the little pool has stirred,
A twig has fallen from the bird,
A twig the linnet homeward bore;
Sh! branch, spread your green canopy o'er—
Sh! now it is fast asleep once more.

FORSAKEN

By Eduard Mörike

Translated from the German by P. H. Thomson

Before the break of day,
 Ere the star beacons dwindle,
The hearth-sticks I must lay,
 The fire kindle.

Bright is the fire's blaze,
 The crackling and blinking;
There I stand and gaze,
 Rapt in my thinking.

Comes then the thought of you
 Suddenly streaming:
Last night, you, boy untrue,
 Came in my dreaming.

Ah! then the teardrops run
 Down unforefended;
So is the day begun—
 O were it ended!

THE SONG

By Arno Holz

Translated from the German by L. M. Kueffner

Over the earth, white clouds are wandering.
    Green through the forest
      flows their light.

          Heart, forget!

  In stillest sunlight
      weaves soothing magic,
'Twixt wind-kissed blossoms blooms thousand-fold balm.

        Forget! forget!

From a distant vale pipes, hearken, a bird. . . .
    It sings its song.

    The song of bliss!
      of bliss.

ON THE LONELY HALLIG

By Detlev von Liliencron

Translated from the Low German by P. H. Thomson

My man is away,
The sea goes high,
My child is sick;
No one to help,
   I am alone.

Her man is home,
The child is dead,
Now in the house
The sick wife lies,
   They are alone.

No doctor near,
No one to help.
The little wife
Is with her child,
   He is alone.

CPSIA information can be obtained
at www.ICGtesting.com
Printed in the USA
BVOW10s2025240417
482142BV00013B/186/P